GROW YOUR OWN MINI FRUIT GARDEN

Planting and Tending Small Fruit Trees

and Berries in Gardens and Containers

CHRISTY WILHELMI

Founder of Gardenerd

COOL
SPRINGS
PRESS

Brimming with creative inspiration, how-to projects, and useful information to enrich your everyday life, Quarto Knows is a favorite destination for those pursuing their interests and passions. Visit our site and dig deeper with our books into your area of interest: Quarto Creates, Quarto Cooks, Quarto Homes, Quarto Lives, Quarto Drives, Quarto Explores, Quarto Gifts, or Quarto Kids.

First Published in 2021 by Cool Springs Press, an imprint of The Quarto Group, 100 Cummings Center, Suite 265-D, Beverly, MA 01915, USA.
T (978) 282-9590 F (978) 283-2742 QuartoKnows.com

Cool Springs Press titles are also available at discount for retail, wholesale, promotional, and bulk purchase. For details, contact the Special Sales Manager by email at specialsales@quarto.com or by mail at The Quarto Group, Attn: Special Sales Manager, 100 Cummings Center, Suite 265-D, Beverly, MA 01915, USA.

25 24 23 22 21   1 2 3 4 5

ISBN: 978-0-7603-7026-1
Digital edition published in 2021

Library of Congress Cataloging-in-Publication Data available

Design: Laura Klynstra
Cover Images: (Front/bottom), (Back/left and right) Emily Murphy; otherwise shutterstock.com
Photography by: Emily Murphy; except Christy Wilhelmi on pages 14 (top), 26 (bottom), 31 (left), 36, 37 (top left), 40, 43 (top right), 45 (top right), 81 (bottom left and right), 84, 89, 103 (top), 123 (top), 153, 163, 171 (left); Whitney Cranshaw, Colorado State University, Bugwood.org on page 164 (right); Eugene E. Nelson, Bugwood.org on page 167 (left); Clemson University—USDA Cooperative Extension Slide Series, Bugwood.org on page 167 (right); and shutterstock.com on pages 14 (bottom), 33 (center), 45 (bottom), 45 (top right), 48, 49 (top), 49 (bottom left), 50, 52, 58, 62 (right), 65 (bottom right), 70, 73 (bottom right), 76 (top), 90, 93 (bottom), 94, 97, 98, 115, 119, 123 (bottom right), 125, 126, 135, 142 (center), 147, 154, 171 (right), 175, 181
Illustration: Holly Neel pages 12, 19, 22, 27, 60, 63, 72, 122, 140-149; otherwise shutterstock.com

Printed in China

DEDICATION

To Andrew Cheeseman, who loves me even though I am "pruning-averse."

CONTENTS

INTRODUCTION

Congratulations on your decision to create a mini fruit garden. What lies ahead is a journey of learning, experimentation, successes, setbacks, and delicious results. This book is organized by tasks: planning and research, preparation, planting, care and tending, harvesting, pruning, and troubleshooting. Feel free to jump forward in these chapters to find the advice you need throughout your adventure. Use the index to your advantage and don't be afraid to dog-ear the pages. Get this book dirty. When you're done, you'll have a new mini fruit garden to show for it.

You'll learn strategies to make the most of your small-space garden and to venture confidently into the unknown. Let the excitement propel you forward and be aware that setbacks are merely . . . setbacks. Your plants may die or become infested with pests; that's okay. This book will help you problem-solve and emerge victorious on the other side. Sometimes that means starting over but remember this: Failure is opportunity. Every gardener, even an expert, experiences failure. Mother Nature is always in charge, and our job is to learn to collaborate with her. Develop your observation skills and listen to nature around you. You'll see more than plants and bugs as you learn. You'll see connections between the sun and leaves, between soil and roots, and so much more. So let's begin this journey together.

Create a space where pollinators thrive, and bees will reward you with fresh fruit.

CHAPTER 1
What's a Mini Fruit Garden?

Not everyone is blessed with acres of land to cultivate and transform into a dream homestead. In fact, most aren't. Most people live on a standard city lot with obstructions from nearby trees and buildings that make it challenging to grow fruiting crops. Factor in amenities such as swimming pools, play areas, storage sheds, and garages, and that doesn't leave much space to work with. With even less space to grow, apartment dwellers make up a significant part of the population, ranging from 6 percent in Mexico, 37 percent in the U.S., to 46 percent in Europe. Those in apartments and condominiums may only have a balcony or porch to utilize. Enter the mini fruit garden.

Mini fruit gardens make the most of whatever space is available. They use strategies such as backyard orchard culture, vertical gardening, multifruit grafting, container planting, espalier techniques, and biointensive methods to grow a rainbow harvest in a small space. While there are limits to what you can grow in a small space, strategic planning will help you exploit the space you have for a tasty and rewarding outcome.

STRATEGIC PLANNING

The first step in planning your mini fruit garden is to assess your space and decide what you have room for. Let's review a few basic design strategies and observation guidelines. Grab a notepad (or graph paper if you want to make notes to scale), pencil, eraser, tape measure, and head outside.

Don't let drafting tools intimidate you. Have fun and explore the possibilities.

SKETCH YOUR SPACE

Draw the outline of your garden area, including any steps or elevation changes. Indicate walls, existing trees, and any element of the space that will remain in place, such as seating areas, barbecues, or play equipment. This will narrow your focus to the space available. Note the dimensions for this available space. This is your canvas.

FINDING NORTH AND SOUTH

Next, figure out where north is (or south in the southern hemisphere). Most mobile devices have compass apps, or you can look up your address on Google Maps. The top of the web page is always north. Once you know where north and south is, you can determine the sun's path across the garden. Refresher: The sun rises in the east and sets in the west. That means the arc of the sun crosses from east to west across the south edge of the sky in the northern hemisphere (north edge of the sky in the southern hemisphere). The sun is lower in winter and nearly straight above in summer. Keep this in mind as you assess sun exposure on your garden. Draw arrows indicating north and south on your design.

Opposite: Planting tallest to shortest from north to south will help full-sun crops get all the light they need.

TALLEST TO SHORTEST

Now that you know where north and south are, you can strategize about tree and shrub placement. The rule of thumb for sun-loving plants is to plant tallest to shortest. Fruit trees and climbing vines should sit north of shorter and trailing plants in the design. To put it simply, tall things cause shade. If you don't want shade, plant the tall stuff north of the shorter stuff. Place low-growing crops such as strawberries farthest south to ensure they will get the sunlight they need to produce fruit.

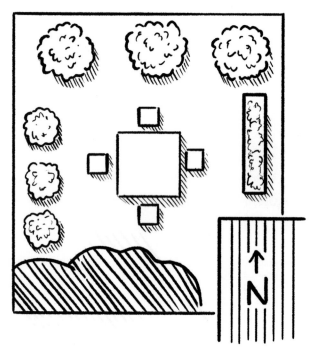

Container fruit trees sit north of blueberries (left) and strawberries (right trough planter) in this patio garden.

Layers of a Food Forest

Another way to utilize the "tallest to shortest" strategy is with a permaculture-style food forest, which is divided into horizontal layers by height. Fruit trees make up the canopy and subcanopy layers above our heads. Plant cane berries, blueberries, and currants as shrub layers or midheight plants, and grow strawberries as a ground cover layer. Most of these have evolved to grow in, and tolerate, partial shade and will do well. Some permaculturists include vining fruits, such as grapes, in their guilds; they can grow up taller trees if they're properly supported.

SPACE HOGS

Make a wish list of the fruits that you want to grow. This is the dream phase so don't hold back. Once you know what crops you want to grow, find out how much room they require. Here's a guide: In-ground fruit trees need to be planted at least 8 feet [2.4 meters] apart or more to allow enough room to grow and to access the harvest (see chapter 3, "Let's Talk Rootstock," for size restrictions). Container-planted fruit trees can be closer together, as close as 4 feet [1.2 meters] apart if the canopy allows, or even closer if planting several trees in the same planting hole (see "Backyard Orchard Culture"). Consult chapter 6 to learn the space requirements for berries and small fruits. Cane berries are called brambles for a reason; they tend to take over so give them plenty of room (3 to 4 feet [.9 to 1.2 meters] on all sides) or contain them to an elevated planter box with a trellis. They are well worth a little chaos for the taste of freshly picked berries steps away from your door.

Give trees enough space to grow with ample access for harvesting.

Place fruit trees and climbing vines in your design first because they are space hogs and will take up the most room. Then use the remaining space to locate fruiting shrubs and ground-trailing plants. Make sure to include pathways—at least 2 feet [.6 meters] wide—between containers and beds. Remember, access is everything. If you can't reach it, you'll feel less inclined to tend your garden. And the local fauna may snatch the harvest before you do.

Raspberries are notorious wanderers. Plan enough space for them and remove runners that pop up in unwanted places.

What's a Stone Fruit?

The stone fruit category consists of fruits that have a pit in the middle. Plums, peaches, nectarines, apricots, apricot hybrids, cherries, mangos, dates, and olives are part of this group. Oddly, cane berries and mulberries are also included, though they do not contain a pit or stone. For the purposes of this book, let's stick with the traditional stone fruits and leave berries for another time.

Four stone fruit trees planted in a single hole demonstrate Backyard Orchard Culture.

BACKYARD ORCHARD CULTURE

What is Backyard Orchard Culture? According to Tom Spellman at Dave Wilson Nursery, Backyard Orchard Culture (BYOC) consists of these four concepts: managing tree size through summer pruning (see "Summer Pruning" in chapter 8) to keep trees small enough to pick fruit without a ladder or at a height that is manageable for the grower; planting fruit trees with staggered harvest periods or successive ripening; planting trees close together in hedgerows or in one cluster to conserve space; and choosing fruit varieties that are adaptable to where you live (see chapter 3), and are, of course, what you actually eat.

MANAGING TREE SIZE

Growing at home is nothing like Commercial Orchard Culture. Why allow a tree to grow out of reach if harvesting will be too difficult when the time comes? Jump to chapters 2 and 8 to learn more about how to choose and train trees to the ideal size for home harvesting.

Keep home orchard fruit trees compact to avoid overgrown branches.

Choosing varieties that produce early, midseason, and late will stagger your harvest through the season.

SUCCESSIVE RIPENING

Backyard Orchard Culture thinks outside the box. Instead of planting one plum that produces fruit for three weeks in summer, you plant two or three varieties that each produce at different times. The yield is lower than commercial production because trees are kept smaller and more accessible, but a lucky gardener can enjoy fruit for months instead of weeks by choosing early, midseason, and late varieties to plant together. Your mini fruit garden can produce all season long or even year-round with the careful calculation of harvest times for each cultivar you choose. But how do you make room for all these varieties? Plant multiple trees in the space of one.

Picture a square shape on the ground that is 2 by 2 feet [.6 by .6 meters]. Imagine a small fruit tree planted on each corner of that square. Spellman suggests planting clusters of trees anywhere from 18 to 24 inches [45 to 61 cm] apart, up to 60 inches [152 cm] apart if you have room. You can plant three to four trees in one big hole or the three to four trees in multiple holes, depending on which is easier for you to dig. For example, the folks at Dave Wilson Nursery suggest planting up to four trees in a 4- by 4-foot [1.2- by 1.2-meter] raised bed. For hedgerows, on

A little planning will prevent a windfall of one fruit at a time.

the other hand, they suggest spacing at least 3 to 5 feet [.9 to 1.5 meters] apart, leaving enough room for proper air circulation. Make sure to allow enough space for adequate canopy growth when planning your design.

If left unchecked, this technique demands more space than a single tree requires. But if you continue to prune the cluster of trees regularly, it can occupy the space of a single tree. Also, to encourage adequate air flow, Spellman recommends thinning the center of the tree grouping, trimming away inward-facing crossing branches that can cause issues as the trees grow inward. We'll cover more on these pruning techniques in chapter 8.

If you want to plant several trees in one hole, or grow a hedgerow of fruit trees, start with one- or two-year-old trees. They will be small, manageable, and easier to prune than established trees. Bare-root fruit trees are inexpensive but require a little planning. ("Bare-root" refers to trees that are sold during their dormant stage with no soil around their roots.) Most nurseries and seed catalogs advertise ordering in fall and early winter depending on the variety and where you live.

Spellman also advises that all the trees in one cluster should be "budded to the same or compatible rootstocks." An example is four successive ripening low-chill apples planted as one combination, each grafted on Mallings 111 rootstock: 'Dorsett Golden' for a summer harvest, 'Gala' for a late summer harvest, 'Fuji' for an early fall harvest, and 'Pink Lady' for a late fall/early winter harvest. That's six months of successive apple harvest all out of the same space as one orchard tree. Find a spot in your yard to plant a hedgerow of stone fruits or a cluster of apple or citrus trees. The rewards will be worth the wait.

Opposite: Choosing the right-sized tree and regular pruning will keep your trees to a manageable size.

Homemade meals from the garden are delicious and fresh. Plant according to what you love to eat.

GROW WHAT YOU'LL EAT

When choosing a fruit tree, make sure it is something everyone in the household will enjoy. If only one person likes quince, maybe everyone will be happy with apples instead. Once you have a list of potential candidates, do your homework and choose the right variety for your hardiness zone, microclimate, and chill hour requirements. Turn to chapter 3 to learn more about those criteria.

Plan for Pollinators

When designing your mini fruit garden, be sure to include space for pollinator-friendly plants including native flowers. After all, 1 out of every 3 to 4 bites of food we eat exists because of the service pollinators provide. Apples, cherries, peaches, plums, some pears, and blueberries require pollinator assistance in order to fruit. To find the best pollinator-friendly plants for your area, visit a local native plant nursery online or in person.

OTHER DESIGN TOOLS

VERTICAL GARDENING

If you can't spread out, go up! Vertical garden systems come in all shapes and sizes, from homemade pallet planters leaning against a sunny wall to high-tech hydroponic towers that boast a bountiful harvest in a 2- to 3-square foot [.6- to .9-square meter] footprint. Before selecting a system, make sure you have the right set-up. Does it require electricity? Do you have an outlet nearby? How will you water it? Is there a hose bib within reach? Does it have to be rotated? Consider the depth of each planting pocket before taking the plunge. Remember, the smaller the pot or soil pocket, the faster it will dry out. If you live in a dry climate, choose a system with deep root zones.

Vertical gardens lend themselves to growing strawberries, thornless bush raspberries, and ground cherries. Strawberries will stay neat and tidy in a vertical garden. The latter two will spill out several feet in all directions.

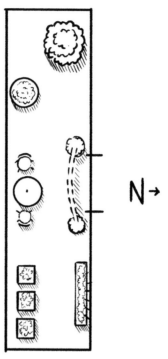

This balcony garden uses a vertical tower to grow strawberries (top left), trellises to keep thornless blackberries in check (bottom right), a space-saving multi-fruit tree (top right), and an arbor to train passion fruit to grow over the door.

Growing towers and vertical gardens are space-saving, especially for low-growing crops such as strawberries.

Eating straight from the garden is possible even when you're growing in small spaces.

These young grape vines are supported by stakes that will soon be replaced with a sturdy arbor.

Arching Ideas

Do you have room overhead for an arbor? Arches, arbors, and pergolas can support vining fruits such as kiwi, dragon fruit, grapes, and passion fruit. Use the space to your advantage to create an overhead fruit source in your garden. Be aware of any shade they may cause and plan accordingly.

Passion fruit make great use of fences, arches, and pergolas in smaller spaces.

MULTI-FRUIT TREES

Some might consider multi-fruit or "fruit salad" trees an abomination of nature, but there's nothing sinister about them. They are a great way to grow three or four different fruits on one tree. Multi-fruit trees are space-saving, funky conversation pieces that will bring diversity to your mini fruit garden. We'll talk more about multi-fruit trees and grafting your own in chapter 4 and, pruning these babies in chapter 8. For now, consider them a biointensive design option as you plan your garden.

ESPALIER

Espalier is a technique dating back to ancient Roman times in which fruit trees were meticulously trained to grow flat against a wall or trellis. It's a perfect solution for a small-space garden. Shaping and training a fruit tree into a flat espalier shape takes time, even years, to develop the right shape from scratch, but nurseries often sell trees that are already espaliered. They cost more due to the labor and time commitment to produce that shape, but if you don't feel like learning how to DIY, buying prefab is an option. See chapter 8 for instructions on how to espalier a young fruit tree.

Opposite Top: Multi-fruit trees grow several fruits of the same genus in one place, like this apple multi-fruit.

Opposite Bottom Left: Espaliered apple trees are shown growing in a narrow pathway.

Opposite Bottom Right: Espaliered fruit trees hug walls so use this space-saving technique in your mini fruit garden.

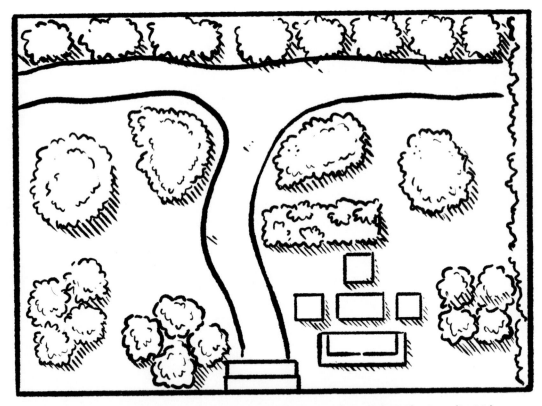

N ↓

This backyard is planted with 4-in-1 stone fruits, citrus, and apples (furthest north). The fig (far left) and pear (far right) are pruned to home-orchard height, while the grapevines hug the wall (right edge), and the blueberry and strawberry patches occupy space toward the south (along center path). Cane berries tolerate shade, so they'll grow well along a shadowed south wall.

COMPLETE YOUR DESIGN

After careful consideration of the available space, sun exposure, ideal plant locations, accessibility, and your crop choices, your design is complete! Now you're ready to bring the design to life. Chapters 2 and 3 will discuss the next steps to ensure a successful garden that will provide you with delicious fruit for years to come.

Opposite: Tuck fruit trees into the corner of your yard or patio to create your mini garden oasis.

Nothing beats a successful harvest from your own garden.

CHAPTER 2

Here's to Your Success!

With a design in hand, you now can begin to prepare your site for planting. Gather your courage, garden tools, and muscle, and let's get to work. This chapter will guide you through the process of selecting the right tree size, preparing the soil for planting, and setting up irrigation for a successful mini fruit garden.

LET'S TALK ROOTSTOCK

Perhaps the most important choice you will make when picking out a fruit tree is size. Not what size tree to *buy*—as in bare-root, 5-gallon [19-liter], 15-gallon [57-liter], or 24-inch [61-cm] box—but what size you want the *mature tree to be*. Size matters in small spaces.

The mature height and spread of a tree are determined in part by the tree's rootstock. Rootstock is the root portion of a grafted tree upon which a scion is grafted. A scion is a small branch of the desired fruit that is cut from one tree and attached to the roots or trunk of another tree. Rootstocks not only help control the size of a tree over time, but they can also provide disease resistance and/or soil tolerance for clayey/sandy or wet/dry conditions. Certain rootstocks allow growers to produce fruit trees that will only mature to as low as 15 percent of a standard tree's height.

Opt to plant younger trees in small spaces. They are more malleable and it is easier to maintain their smaller size as they grow in.

Most fruit trees are labeled as standard, semi-dwarf, or dwarf. Some are available as very-dwarf or miniature. Here's the breakdown:

- Standard fruit trees will grow to a mature height of 15 to 25 feet [4.5 to 7.6 meters] tall
- Semi-dwarf trees will grow to between 50 to 75 percent of standard height, 12 to 15 feet [3.6 to 4.5 meters] tall
- Dwarf trees will grow to between 30 to 50 percent of standard height, 8 to 10 feet [2.4 to 3 meters] tall
- Very-dwarf or miniature trees grow to between 15 to 30 percent of standard height and may be hard to find

Bare-root fruit trees arrive dormant and are a great starting size for small gardens.

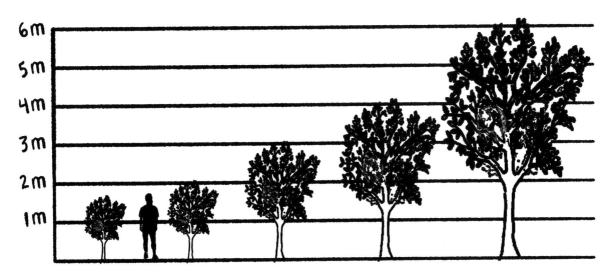

6m
5m
4m
3m
2m
1m

Mature tree size is determined by rootstock. Choose wisely based on your available space.

Check nursery stock for circling roots.

Shopping Tip

When shopping for fruit trees at a nursery, don't be shy about removing the rootball from the nursery pot to inspect it for circling or girdled roots. Look for roots growing above the soil line; that's a clear sign of girdling below. Avoid trees with roots making a sharp curve circling the trunk.

It becomes obvious right away that the best choice for a mini fruit garden is a tree with dwarf or very-dwarf rootstock, with semi-dwarf as a close third. Remember, the canopy of a tree grows as wide as it is tall. Keep that in mind when planning your garden. Pruning also plays a huge role in maintaining tree size, but we'll get to that in chapter 8.

There are recommended rootstocks for each family of fruit trees at every size. In other words, one size does not fit all. See the "Rootstock Chart" in Appendix A for detailed options. More advanced gardeners can acquire rootstock to graft their own scions at home. Newbies may want to stick to what's offered at nurseries. Either way, choose the smallest size for your garden to ensure room for more than one tree.

Dwarf and semi-dwarf fruit trees work
well in small front yard mini orchards.

Happy trees grow in happy soil. Soil preparation is the key to abundant harvests.

PREPARING THE SOIL

Times have changed, and while at one point, experts recommended adding plenty of soil amendments to the planting hole before placing the tree, the current science shows that trees do best when planted in native soil. Think about it—if you fill a hole the size of a 15-gallon [57-liter] pot with rich compost and organic fruit tree fertilizer, tree roots have no motivation to grow beyond that amended area and out into native soils. Trees end up stunted over time. It's better, instead, to amend a larger area, and more importantly, enhance your native Soil Food Web population to improve drainage, increase nutrient accessibility, and boost disease resistance. What's the Soil Food Web? Glad you asked.

SOIL FOOD WEB

Picture a network of microscopic organisms living in your soil. That's the FBI—fungi, bacteria, and insects. They consume organic matter (such as mulch and compost) and exudates (sugars) from tree and other plant roots and put them to work. They also perform a multitude of functions. Sugar-filled bacteria become food for other organisms such as protozoa and nematodes (our nutrient cyclers). Those nutrient cyclers convert substances into food that plants and tree roots can use immediately. Fungi form long chains, reaching deep into soils to extract minerals and nutrients far below root systems, bringing those nutrients and minerals back to plant and tree roots. Fungi also work with the larger members of the Soil Food Web—micro-arthropods, arthropods, and worms—to break up and aerate compacted soils, doing the work for you to improve drainage. Use nature's task force to do the bulk of your soil preparation. Here's how.

If your soil is poorly draining clay, it is imperative to loosen the soil and amend the overall area to break up the clay's structure. Otherwise compacted soils invite diseases including those mentioned under "Viruses and Other Pathogen Diseases" in chapter 9. In many cases, good soil prep is the only treatment (read: preventative method) for diseases caused by poor drainage or compaction. Flip ahead to peruse the diseases mentioned in chapter 9 to determine whether any of them is prevalent in your area. If so, pay careful attention to the following pages.

If you're willing to plan ahead, you can try the following method for increasing soil permeability instead of tilling (which destroys the Soil Food Web, BTW). Put down a layer of microbially rich compost and top it with a 3- to 5-inch [7.5- to 13-cm] layer of bark chips. Keep it well watered and wait. Within a few months soil microbes will break down the mulch and integrate the compost on your behalf. Your soil will be aerated, it will drain better, and you'll find it easier to dig that planting hole. Nature does the work so both you and your trees will be happier in this environment.

Water is a key component to keep soil microbes happy. When soils become dry, microbes go dormant or die. Mulch helps retain moisture and feeds microbes, so keep your soil covered and irrigated as you prepare the bed for planting.

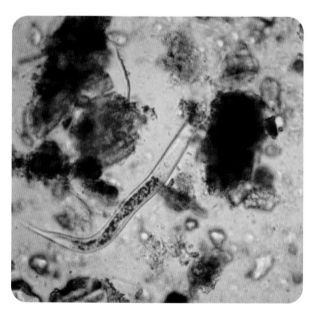

Bacteria, fungi, and other helpful members of the Soil Food Web as seen under a microscope.

Earthworms tunnel and aerate soils, while depositing nutrient-rich castings along the way.

Brew Compost Tea

Aerated compost tea is made by "brewing" compost in a mesh bag in a large bucket of filtered water. A pump bubbles oxygen throughout the bucket, which ensures that the right type of microbes (aerobic) breed rather than the wrong type (anaerobic). Microbes require food, usually fish hydrolysate, kelp meal, and humic acids, in order to multiply and grow properly. The whole ensemble brews for 18 to 24 hours, then must be applied within 2 to 4 hours, lest the microbes die without additional food and aeration. Compost tea can be applied via foliar spray or soil drench. It can also be diluted to cover more terrain. To properly brew your own compost tea at home you'll need:

- 1 5-gallon [19-liter] bucket
- 1 air pump for 5 gallons [19 liters]
- Tubing for the pump
- 1 mesh bag (400-micron mesh) with a clamp to affix the bag to the bucket
- Filtered water

INGREDIENTS FOR WHAT GOES IN THE BAG:
- ½ pound [225 grams] biologically active compost or Arctic humus
- Fish hydrolysate (or a vegan alternative)
- Soluble kelp meal
- Optional additions include insect frass, alfalfa meal, and humic acids

To make a brew, fill the bucket with filtered water until it's 2 inches [5 cm] from the top. Add a couple drops of humic acids to break the bonds of chlorine and chloramine if you don't have a water filter. Place compost, kelp meal, and other granular additions (alfalfa or insect frass) to the mesh bag. Follow package instructions for recommended amounts. Mix fish hydrolysate or a vegan alternative with water in the bucket until it's thoroughly dissolved. Place the mesh bag and air pump tubing in the bucket; you may need to clamp both into place. Put the lid loosely on the bucket. Plug in the pump and brew for no more than 18 to 24 hours. By then, microbes will have multiplied and consumed the foods in the mixture. After 18 to 24 hours, unplug the pump, remove the compost (add it to your compost bin), and thoroughly clean your equipment. Leave no biofilm or residue behind. Biofilms affect future batches of compost tea (biofilms breed anaerobic bacteria, folks!). Apply the compost tea to garden beds, fruit trees, cane berries, and elsewhere as needed. You can dilute the mixture to cover more area. Some gardeners use a 4:1 water to compost tea ratio for soil drenching but use it full strength for foliar spray. Use a pump or backpack sprayer to apply a foliar spray to all leaf surfaces. Make sure to spray the undersides of leaves too! That's where many plants take in nutrients.

Compost tea is a wonderful addition to any soil care practice.

Aerated compost tea (see the "Brew Compost Tea" sidebar) is another way to add billions of beneficial microbes to your soil. Apply aerated compost tea on top of the mulch layer as a soil drench. The added microbes will feed on the mulch, work their way down into the native soil, and bring your soil back to life. If you don't have time or the inclination to brew your own compost tea, search the web for trustworthy sources of beneficial microbes. You can also search for "compost tea service" to find a provider near you.

COMPLETING SOIL PREP

If your soil is ready to dig, turn to chapter 5 for the best way to dig the hole and plant the tree. If you don't want to wait for nature's helpers to lighten the workload, grab your digging fork, a load of compost, and get a great workout. Spread compost on the soil surface and turn it into the soil with the digging fork. Work compost into the entire garden area down to 12 inches [30 cm] if possible, rather than just the future location for your tree. Remember, roots travel as wide as the aboveground canopy. Your planting hole for the tree will most likely be deeper than 12 inches [30 cm], but feeder roots are more superficial and will benefit from amendments at this depth. If soil-borne diseases are prevalent in your area, seriously consider sending a sample to a soil lab for pathogen testing.

TEST FOR DRAINAGE

Clay soils drain poorly, which lead to drowning if tree roots sit in water too long. Test your soil for adequate drainage with this procedure:

Dig a hole 12 inches [30 cm] deep and wide. Fill the hole with water and wait overnight. The water should be drained by morning. Fill the hole again and wait. If after 3 to 4 hours the hole still has standing water, it's time to consider a raised bed for planting. Raised beds "rise above" soil drainage problems because you can mix native soil in with ample amounts of compost to break up clay soil structure. Over time the added compost will work its way down into the clay soil below and increase porosity and drainage as roots grow.

It is essential to test for drainage before planting. Don't skip this important step.

Whether they're planted in-ground or in containers, fruit is in your future.

GROWING FRUIT TREES IN CONTAINERS

As discussed earlier in this chapter, rootstock regulates mature tree size. When growing in containers, dwarf and miniature fruit trees are the best choices to keep both you and your trees happy. But let's back up to review the ideal container specifications for growing fruit trees.

CHOOSE YOUR CONTAINER

First and foremost, the happiness of your fruit tree begins with choosing the right size container. When planted in the ground, fruit tree roots often mirror the aboveground growth in depth and spread. In a container, roots can't spread out so give them as much room as possible. Whether you purchase a bare-root, or a 5-, 7-, or 15-gallon [19-, 26.5-, 57-liter] potted tree, your container should be larger than the original nursery pot to accommodate future growth. Start with the biggest pot you can afford, ideally a minimum of 22 to 24 inches [55 to 61cm] in diameter and height. Half-whiskey barrels also serve the purpose, although they drain well (possibly too well) and

may require more frequent watering. If you expect to move your tree up to a larger pot as it grows, avoid containers with tapered rims. It will be difficult to remove the rootball, and you will have to sacrifice the pot to do so.

This loquat tree has outgrown its pot and needs to be transplanted.

Opposite: Half-wine barrels make great containers for fruit trees.

Urn-shaped containers will make transplanting up to a larger pot difficult. Stick with tapered or straight containers or be prepared to break the pot when it's time to transplant.

Air Pruning

Fabric pots and slatted containers, similar to plastic laundry baskets, help keep container trees and shrubs happy through air pruning. Air pruning occurs when roots are exposed to oxygen. The root tips dry and stop growing. That sounds like a bad thing, but it actually triggers more root development without overgrowing the pot. You may need to water more often, but your trees will self-prune their roots to stay content in their pots.

Plastic containers tend to be less expensive but can become brittle over time and crack under pressure as a rootball expands. Terracotta containers are generally less expensive but are sturdier. Wooden containers are a beautiful solution and are usually less expensive than ceramic and stone. Ceramic and stone containers cost more but are more durable over the life of the tree.

Weight is also a factor. If you plan to move the tree from time to time, choose the lightest container available. If you live in a climate where wind is fierce and frequent, choose a heavier pot to anchor the tree. No one enjoys fishing fruit trees out of the swimming pool after a windy day.

No matter what type of container you choose, there is one fact to become familiar with: Fruit tree roots eventually grow through the container's drainage hole. If you place your potted fruit tree container on soil, the roots will inevitably find their way through the pot's drainage holes to soil, more water, and nutrient sources if you let them. To prevent this, consider placing a saucer underneath the pot at planting time. Otherwise, somewhere down the line, you may have to break the pot to save the tree, roots and all.

Opposite: Ceramic, terracotta, plastic, and wood are all container options for your mini fruit garden.

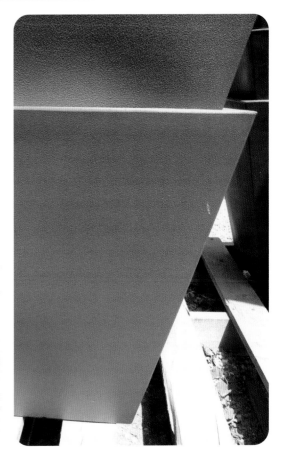

A successful fruit harvest requires proper irrigation as the plant is getting established and during times of drought.

IRRIGATION

Mní wičhóni is the Lakota way of saying, "Water is life." Every fruit tree, and even cacti, needs water in order to produce succulent fruits. Without proper irrigation our dreams of a bountiful harvest evaporate. The key to watering fruit trees is to water deeply but infrequently. Fruit trees and fruiting shrubs require less frequent irrigation than most annual vegetable and fruit crops because they have deep perennial root systems. Fruit trees generally don't like to be on the same watering schedule as lawns, which are often watered several times per week for short periods of time—the exact opposite of what trees want. As trees mature, the frequency (or watering schedule) reduces as the duration (length of time irrigating) increases. A new fruit tree may want a good soak once per week, but in a year, it will have a deeper root system that prefers a longer soak every two to three weeks instead. Mature trees need water only once per month when planted in-ground.

Your soil conditions will dictate the frequency and duration of your irrigation schedule. There is no single answer to the question, "How much should I water?" If you do the drainage test described in this chapter, you will learn a lot about your soil and have a better idea of the watering duration and frequency that's appropriate for your property.

When growing in containers, the schedule mentioned here is less concrete. Depending on the material of your container, you may need to water two times per week or more in extreme heat/dry climates. If you get summer rains, you may never need to irrigate.

HAND-WATERING CONTAINER TREES

A good rule of thumb when watering containers is to irrigate until you see water flow from the drainage hole. But be aware that if dry soil has pulled away from the sides, water may rush to the bottom of the pot without soaking the rootball. Water slowly and gently at first to ensure it is absorbed.

Observe how quickly moisture evaporates from your chosen container by using a moisture meter. Basic models are available at most nurseries and from online garden catalogs. High-tech moisture meters can be calibrated to give a more accurate reading. Test daily after watering to ensure the entire rootball is moist to a depth of 12 inches [30 cm] and to see how many days pass before the rootball dries.

DRIP IRRIGATION

Drip irrigation is a time-saving investment that delivers water slowly at soil level. Drip systems are far more efficient than sprinklers because they deposit water right where it is needed, losing less to evaporation and runoff. Battery operated timers, available at hardware stores, attach easily to a hose spigot. You can run ½-inch [1-cm] drip tubing behind a row of containers and connect individual ¼-inch [.6-cm] tubes with bubblers leading to each container. Think of drip irrigation as a puzzle; if you have all the pieces, it's easy to complete. There is a series of connectors, end plugs, and adapters that allows you to build your drip system from end to end. Here is an example of how to connect the pieces together:

To a hose spigot connect → plumber's tape → battery-operated timer (pressure reducer and filter screen optional) → plumber's tape → hose-end-to-½-inch [1-cm] adaptor → ½-inch [1 cm] tubing with no emitters (running the length of a container row) → ½-inch [1-cm] end cap.

Then, along the length of the ½-inch [1-cm] tube use a drip irrigation hole punch tool to create openings to insert your ¼-inch [.6-cm] tubes. Next, insert ¼-inch [.6-cm] barbed connectors → ¼-inch [.6-cm] tubing with no emitters → spider bubbler with stake.

Stake the spider bubbler in the container and adjust the volume of flow to ensure even coverage and adequate watering. Turn on the hose spigot and test all lines and connections for leaks. Adjust the pressure at the hose spigot to prevent blowouts at the connecting points (too much pressure can cause frequent and unpleasant geysers in the garden). Leave the spigot on at all times; the battery-operated timer has a valve that will shut off and turn on the flow as scheduled.

That's it!

This battery-operated system can be used for in-ground plantings as well, or you can convert existing sprinklers to drip with a little help from an expert. Instead of bubblers, use tubing with emitters—prefab holes in the tubing every 6, 10, or 12 inches [15, 25.5, or 30 cm]—for in-ground trees. Coil drip tubing with emitters around the tree, starting 1 foot [30 cm] away from the trunk. Spiral the tubing along the tree's root zone with 1 foot [30 cm] spacing, continuing outward toward the edge of the canopy, which is also known as the drip line.

Plan your irrigation as you plan your garden design. If possible, group similarly sized or aged trees together to ensure adequate watering. If that is not an option, you may need to hand-water smaller or younger plants in-between scheduled waterings, but the bulk of the work will be automatic.

Now you're on your way! You have containers at the ready or you're working on your in-ground soil prep and irrigation strategy. Now it's time to choose the right fruit varieties for your garden. Chapter 3 will guide you toward the best options.

Get off to a great start by choosing the right tree for your space.

CHAPTER 3

Choosing the Best Fruit Trees for Your Climate

Whether you are a novice or an experienced gardener, the first rule applies to everyone: Choose cultivars best suited to where you live. After all, the goal is an abundant fruit garden, right? Planting a fruit tree that is appropriate for your growing region, microclimate, and chill hours is the key to success. What a shame it would be to plant a tree, and then wait five, ten, even fifteen years and never see a single fruit. It has been known to happen but is far less likely to occur if you choose the right varieties for your climate. Let's dive into the checklist of fruit tree qualifications.

Gardeners in warm-winter climates can grow avocados without risk of frost damage.

HARDINESS ZONE

Hardiness zones run close to the latitude lines of our planet, grouping areas with similar temperature averages and frost dates into specific zones. These zones reveal the average extreme minimum temperature both in degrees Fahrenheit and degrees Centigrade. In other words, they tell you how cold it gets in each zone. Hardiness zones start with zone 1 at the poles, with an average minimum temperature of below -50°F [-45.5°C] and increases in warmth toward the equator to zone 13, with lows around 59°F [15°C]. Seed catalogs and nurseries use hardiness zones to alert gardeners to the specific fruit trees and shrubs that will grow best in their zone. Some companies won't sell live plants to regions outside of recommended hardiness zones, or they will waive replacement guarantees before shipping. Berries and fruit trees that are "not frost tolerant" are best suited to warm-winter climates.

For example, an avocado tree is generally listed as being safe to grow in zones where the average minimum temperatures don't fall below 10°F [-12°C]. If you live where winter temperatures drop to -10°F [-23°C], you might want to skip planting an avocado tree. Or if you're adventurous, grow it in a well-insulated greenhouse sited where it gets plenty of full sun, surrounded by drums of water (which will keep greenhouses warmer in winter) and see what happens.

Every continent across the globe has its own system of hardiness zones. Ask your local nursery to help you determine your zone in your respective country.

Picking the right trees for your hardiness zone prevents sadness and unwanted mourning over fruit trees lost to frost damage.

Fruit-bearing olive trees can be grown for oil or brining in warm-winter hardiness zones.

Pears are ideal fruit trees for cold-winter climates.

Fruits for Chilly Places

If you live in a northern (or southern in the southern hemisphere) or mountainous region, consider growing apples, cane berries, cherries, currants, pears, and stone fruits. They have high chill hour requirements that won't be a concern where you live.

MICROCLIMATES

Within those hardiness zones there are pockets of microclimates—climates that differ from the registered norms of the area. A house tucked into a forested canyon may be in one designated hardiness zone, but it might get much colder and windier there than its neighbors 100 yards [91 meters] away on the ridge in full sun. Your own backyard has microclimates too! That corner by the back wall that bakes in the hot summer is a different microclimate than the nook under the oak tree. Use these microclimates to your advantage. Fruit trees and berries that require more chill hours (see the following "Chill Hours" section and chart) may thrive in that nook if it gets enough sun throughout the day. Take time to explore your growing space to find the different microclimates. This will help you strategize the best locations for growing fruits.

Blueberries tolerate partial shade and work well when grown in chilly corners of the garden.

Asian pears are satisfying to grow at home.

Fruits for Warm Spots

If you live in a warm-winter climate where temperatures don't drop below 20°F [-6.6°C], you can grow all citrus fruits and subtropical fruits including avocados, figs, guavas, mulberries, olives, and pomegranates. Look for low-chill varieties of stone fruits, apples, and blueberries.

CHILL HOURS

One of the most important factors to consider when selecting a fruit tree is the tree's chilling requirements. What are chill hours and how do we get them? The term "chill hours" is defined as the annual number of hours when temperatures are below 45°F [7.2°C] during a tree's dormancy period. If you want to get more technical, some specialists say chill hours are measured in hours between 32°F [0°C] to 45°F [7.2°C]. It is also said that temperatures over 60°F [15.5°C] during dormancy are subtracted from total annual winter chill hours. But let's keep it simple. Deciduous trees will not produce fruit (or will produce very few) if they don't first go through a dormancy period where their requirement for chill hours is met.

For example, let's say you want to grow pears. Chilling requirements for pear varieties range from 200–1,000 chill hours. That means different cultivars need between 200–1,000 hours of temperatures below 45°F [7.2°C] in one winter season in order to produce flowers and fruit the following spring. Asian pears and some newer cultivars sit on the low end, requiring only 200–400 chill hours, but most pears need 600 chill hours or more. Hence, the best location for growing pears is a cold or mountainous region that receives at least 600 chill

Some fruits require cold weather or they won't produce fruit. Each tree has a chilling requirement, with some available in low-chill varieties.

Winter chill brings fruit in spring.

hours for success. Gardeners in warm-winter regions should seek out low-chill varieties that will produce fruit in conditions with minimal chill hours. Coastal climates tend to have moderate temperatures with fewer extremes, and therefore fewer chill hours. The ocean buffers nearby landmasses from plummeting temperatures in winter. Gardeners in cold-winter climates need not worry about chill hours (you'll get plenty of them) but should instead focus on durability and frost tolerance when selecting fruit trees.

Now for the fun part, which is deciding what fruits will grow best in your climate. First, find out how many chill hours your growing region receives in a year. You can do that by searching the internet for "chill hours calculator (your city, region, state, or province)." Many university agriculture departments around the world have calculators that allow you to type in your city name or postal code, and the calculator provides you with averages. Be aware, as climate change affects our areas, hardiness zones are shifting. Places that used to receive 300–500 chill hours may now get only 150–250. Times are changing, and we must adapt our mini fruit gardens to accommodate these shifts.

Gooseberries typically require high chill hours but low-chill varieties are available.

Here are some common fruits and the range of chill hours they require. Note: LC = Low Chill cultivars.

FRUIT TYPE	TYPICAL CHILL HOUR RANGE	NOTES
Apple	500–1,000	LC 300–500
Avocado	No chill requirement	Not frost tolerant
Blueberry	500–1,000	LC 150–400
Cane berry (blackberry, raspberry, and so forth.)	500–1,200	LC 0–300
Cherry	500–700	LC 250–400
Citrus	No chill requirement	Not frost tolerant
Currant and Gooseberry	800–1,200	LC 200–300
Fig	100–300	Not frost tolerant
Guava	100	Not frost tolerant
Mulberry	200–450	Some hardy to -30°F [-34.4°C]
Olive	150–300	Frost resistant above 20°F [-6.6°C]
Peach/Nectarine/Plum/Apricot	800–1,000	LC 250–500
Pear	600–1,000	LC 200–400
Pomegranate	100–200	Not frost tolerant
Quince	100–500	Some hardy to -20°F [-29°C]
Strawberry	200–400	Chilled after harvest

Fire blight is common in many fruit trees. Quickly identify and remove affected leaves. Be sure to sterilize pruning shears between cuts.

OTHER CONSIDERATIONS

Once you determine your hardiness zone, find your microclimates, and discover how many chill hours your garden receives, it's time to pick varieties to grow. Here are three more things to consider as you select varieties.

DISEASE RESISTANCE

As mentioned, choice of rootstock can offer some disease resistance in fruit tree varieties. Before choosing which fruits you want to grow, check around for diseases common in your area. Peach leaf curl, powdery mildew, fire blight, scab, crown rot, and bacterial canker may be prevalent where you live. Some diseases are manageable with the right rootstock, while others affect trees after planting regardless of its inherent resistance. Those issues are treated seasonally with horticultural and dormant sprays, and other methods we'll discuss in chapter 9. If you know your soil has soilborne diseases or drainage issues, make sure to select a tree on hearty rootstock that resists crown and root rot.

FRUITING SEASON

We touched on this in chapter 2 under "Backyard Orchard Culture," but it's worth repeating. Before purchasing a fruit tree, berry, or other fruit producer, find out when that tree, shrub, or vine is productive and for how long. Cherry and apricot season can be over before you blink, whereas citrus and avocados produce for several months. If you select multiple varieties that produce early, midseason, or late fruit you can extend the harvest over a longer period of time. Gardeners who lack the room for more than one variety of a single fruit should try to plan a garden that produces each crop at a different time to stagger the abundance, for example, blueberries followed by blackberries, then citrus, then apples. You will see and taste the seasons as they pass.

In coastal and humid climates, powdery mildew is a common issue.

Stone fruit trees can become infected with peach leaf curl. Well-timed applications of dormant oils and pruning help prevent it.

Organic dormant oils protect trees from some insects and diseases that take hold during budbreak and early spring.

Two different cherry trees help each
other become more abundant in spring.

Apples, cherries, and pears benefit from pollinators and pollinizer trees nearby.

POLLINATION

Some fruit trees are considered "self-fruitful," meaning they don't require another fruit tree nearby in order to set fruit. Citrus, figs, nectarines, peaches, persimmons, and some plums and apricots are self-fruitful. Most, but not all, cherries, pears, and apples, on the other hand, require the pollen of a compatible cultivar of the same species in order to fruit successfully. This compatible cultivar is often referred to as a "pollinizer," a plant that is known to provide pollen for another. For example, a 'Minnie Royal' cherry requires a 'Royal Lee' cherry nearby as a pollinizer. 'Bosc' pears will pollinize 'Bartlett', 'd'Anjou', 'Comice', or 'Seckel' varieties, and vice versa. Even self-fertile fruits, such as blueberries, benefit from having a different variety close by to increase productivity. Find out whether your dream fruit tree is self-fruitful or not. Most nurseries and seed catalogs note "self-fruitful" or list the required pollinizer for each one.

For small-space gardeners, it's important to strategize and design a plan that uses every square inch effectively. The varieties you choose and their fruiting season play into this strategy. Are you limited to a patio garden? Find your favorite fruits in dwarf sizes to accommodate those limits. Do you have a long wall or fence you'd like to utilize? Consider espalier or vining fruit crops. Is this your forever garden or just a temporary one? The answer helps you determine what materials to choose. If you need to circle back to chapters 1 and 2 to modify your design, go for it. Nothing is etched in stone. Take your time to plot the location for each crop. When it feels right, you're ready to move on to chapter 4.

Citrus blossoms attract bees and other pollinators. Their aroma fills any mini fruit garden with sweet fragrance.

Figs start small but end with big flavor in a mini fruit garden.

Four scaffold branches, each a different variety, have been grafted onto a single trunk for increased biodiversity in a small-space garden.

CHAPTER 4

Grafted Trees and Their Importance to Small-Scale Home Orchards

You've already learned how grafting a desired fruit scion onto a selected rootstock restricts a tree's mature size. But grafting is a technique used for more than rootstock. Grafting dates back thousands of years, and is, in fact, how many of the fruits we enjoy today still exist. Why is this? Let's talk about plant sex for a moment.

WHY ARE TREES GRAFTED?

As mentioned in chapter 3, fruit trees require pollination to produce a fruit. You know the basics: male flower parts pollinate female flower parts, the same as what happens with many vegetable crops. Most fruit trees are monoecious, meaning the male and female parts share the same flower (aka, perfect flowers), while other monoecious trees have separate male and female flowers (imperfect flowers). Some trees take a different approach entirely. They have A and B flowers that are both male and female, but at different times of the day. Crazy! But let's stay focused.

Once pollination occurs, a fruit forms. But the seed inside that fruit has a genetic past. It contains the history of all the genetic material that came in contact with that flower during bloom. Bees and other pollinators traffic pollen from flower to flower without regard for which cultivar it is. Therefore, that seed contains genetic material from other varieties or even other members of the same plant family. If you try to plant that seed and grow a new tree from it, the result will most likely be different from the mother fruit. Seeds inside fruits are wildcards that don't grow true to type. This process is called sexual reproduction.

Enter grafting. Grafting is *asexual* reproduction. By taking a cutting (a scion) from a tree and attaching it to rootstock or another tree in the same family, the fruit that grows from that scion will be just like its mother fruit. The genetic identity is true to type. Grafting promotes consistency in a tree's overall traits, such as when it blooms and when it fruits. It is an indispensable practice that perpetuates most of our favorite fruit varieties.

Opposite: The heirloom apples we enjoy today wouldn't exist without grafting.

NOW, ABOUT THOSE MULTI-FRUIT TREES

A multi-fruit is simply a tree with two to five types of fruits in the same family (e.g., all stone fruits) grafted to the trunk of a single tree. For example, a multi-fruit stone fruit tree includes one grafted branch—or scion—each of a plum, nectarine, peach, and apricot. They are all stone fruits, and they are all growing together from one trunk.

The grafted scion becomes part of the tree once the graft union heals and it will grow as if it belonged to the mother tree all along. Each variety is grafted to grow in a different direction, so you'll have plums in one direction, peaches in the opposite direction, and apricots and nectarines growing between the other two.

Multi-fruit stone fruit and apple trees are usually grouped by chill hours. For example, a low-chill multi-fruit apple tree might have one or two branches each of 'Anna', 'Fuji', 'Dorsett Golden', and 'Pink Lady' varieties grafted to one trunk. These cultivars all require fewer than 500 chill hours. Citrus trees are also available in multi-fruit options, in combinations of lemons, limes, tangerines, grapefruits, and pomelos. To plant four trees in one planting hole, à la Backyard Orchard Culture in chapter 1, multi-fruit trees allow mini fruit gardeners to enjoy more than one variety in the space of one tree. Newbie gardeners can purchase pre-grafted multi-fruit trees for citrus, stone fruits, pears, cherries, and apples. More advanced gardeners can create their own multi-fruit trees by grafting scions to existing trees.

Fresh apples from the garden are great for eating or baking.

Word to the Wise

When planting a multi-fruit tree, take note of any identifying tags or paint on each branch. These tell you which variety is associated with each scion. Resist the urge to remove the tags lest you lose track of each fruit's location. Tags become even more important when pruning, to avoid cutting off too much of one variety's fruiting wood. If you find them unsightly, you can match each fruit to a paint color and reapply as the paint fades each year.

Opposite: Avocado trees have either A or B flowers, but some hybrids are self-fruitful.

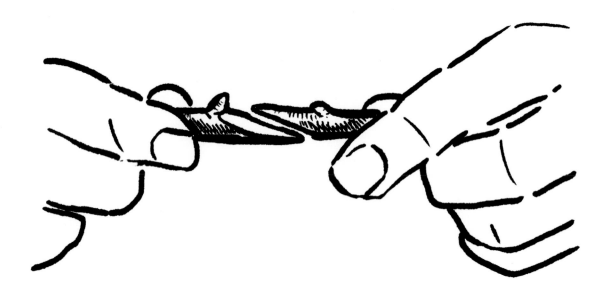

A splice graft is easy with the right tools and training.

GRAFTING BASICS

Let's say you want to create your own multi-fruit trees. Or maybe you want to improve pollination and fruiting of an existing fruit tree. If you said *Yes!* to either of these ideas, then grafting may be for you. As a small space gardener, you may not have room for both a 'Minnie Royal' and a 'Royal Lee' cherry tree, which are required to grow together for adequate pollination. If that's the case, consider grafting a pollinizer of one tree onto the other. Graft a scion of 'Minnie Royal' onto 'Royal Lee' and you'll see fruit in the coming years with only one tree. This technique works on young trees, typically in their first or second year.

Keep in mind, however, that grafting is a more advanced skill that you can acquire once you feel ready to take the leap. Here is some guidance for your journey.

A few choice tools and a bit of knowledge will equip you for your grafting journey.

TOOLS OF THE TRADE

First, choose the best grafting knife you can afford. A grafting knife is sharp, short, and beveled on one side. That means there are right-handed and left-handed knives available, if you want to use your dominant hand. Many blades are combination budding/grafting tools in one. Fancier tools look more like a hole-punch or a wrench. These tools cut a perfect "V" or other interlocking shape in both the scion and host branch so they slide together like a snug-fitting puzzle piece when joined. They take the guesswork out of cutting an identical angle on two separate pieces.

Other important materials for this task include grafting tape, a sharpening tool to keep your blade at peak performance level, a wedge, possibly a hammer, and wax for nooks too difficult to wrap with tape. Biodegradable or poly tapes seal up the union until bark heals around it. Wedges help keep a cut open until you insert the scion. In situations working with older rootstock, the hammer comes in handy with that wedge. Wax provides protection against moisture as the union heals. You may not need all of these for every project, but they are good to have around when you do. One last tool to have at the ready is a first aid kit. Even experienced grafters can end up in the emergency room when a grafting knife misses its target.

HOW GRAFTING WORKS

Grafting feels a bit like magic, but it is simply science and nature beautifully combined. When the cambium layer of a tree—the layer of cells just below the bark—is exposed, that exposure can damage the tree. But if you insert a cutting with *its* cambium layer exposed, the two will become one in time. According to the University of California Agriculture and Natural Resources, the cambium layer has "actively dividing. . .undifferentiated *callus* cells" that "soon differentiate into new vascular tissues that permit the passage of nutrients and water between the stock and the scion." If all goes according to plan, the union heals and the scion is accepted by the tree as one of its own. There are myriad ways to attach new fruiting wood to host trees or rootstocks, but here are the most common in use.

SPLICE GRAFTING

David King of The Learning Garden in Los Angeles, California, teaches grafting classes for the University of California Los Angeles. He suggests thinking of the cambium layer as a tube. When splice grafting, the goal is to make contact between the tubes of both pieces. The simple way to accomplish that is to cut the scion wood and the host wood at the same 20-degree angle. The two pieces should be as close in diameter as possible, too, so that the two cambium tubes line up directly. The longer and more angled the cut, say 2 inches [5 cm] at 20 degrees rather than a ½ inch [1 cm] at 45 degrees, the more cambium is exposed. The more cambium, the better the chances are for connection. Once joined, the graft is wrapped with tape or covered with wax to heal. Splice grafting can be done during dormancy through early spring.

Grafting begins with a cleanly cut scion and host branch.

When a scion "takes," it begins to leaf out as an accepted part of the tree.

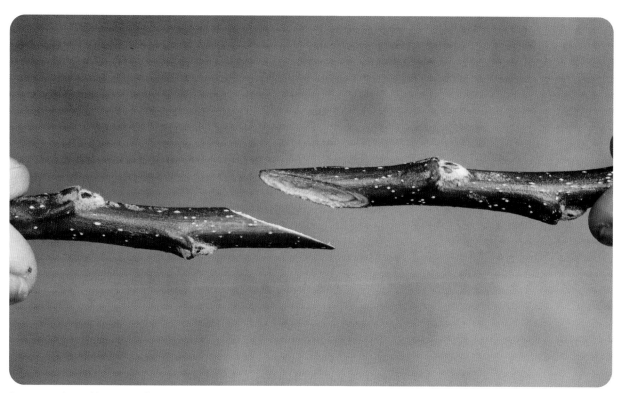

A steeper angle provides more surface area for scions to attach to a host branch.

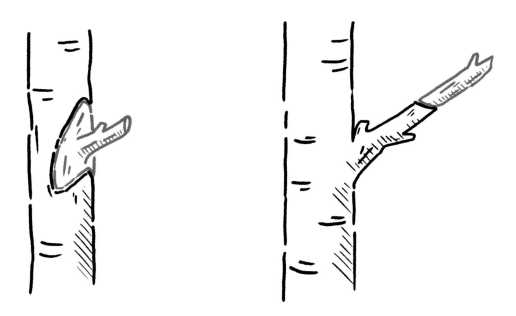

You can see the difference between a bud graft (left) vs. a scion graft. Both are used to increase fruit production and diversity, but the timing for each is different.

BUD GRAFTING

Budding—or bud grafting—is a technique used primarily by nursery professionals and more advanced gardeners. Instead of attaching a scion or branch cutting to a tree, the grafter inserts a smaller section of the branch containing a single or double bud into a cutout on the host tree. The shape of the cutting exposes more of the cambium layer of both parts. Bud grafting is great for trees that don't experience leaf drop or outright dormancy, such as citrus. There are two methods to choose from when bud grafting: T-budding or chip budding.

T-BUDDING

With T-budding, the grafter cuts a "T" in the bark of the host tree and slides the budwood, shaped like an oblong family crest, into the pocket between the bark and cambium layer. This kind of grafting is best done while the tree is growing and the bark is "slipping," or peels away easily from the tree. Depending on where you live, tree slipping occurs in spring, summer, and very early fall. If your plans do not overlap with an ideal time to T-bud, consider using the chip budding method instead.

CHIP BUDDING

Chip budding is perfect for grafting during late summer, fall, or during the dormant season. King describes the process: On the host tree, make an indented cut about 3-4 inches (7.5-10 cm) long. At the base of the graft cut an indentation, a shelf of sorts, to secure the bottom part of the bud in place. Insert the bud into the indentation, then secure it with grafting tape. This technique is used to graft grapevines as well.

Both grafting and budding require practice, and success is not always guaranteed. King's advice for new grafters is, "Don't rush, take it easy. Expect to fail and keep that sharp edge of the blade pointed away from you." He speaks from experience when he suggests cutting away from yourself at all times. If possible, use a surface to cut the scion, rather than bracing against your thumb. Once you get the hang of it the result, when it works, is magical.

Opposite Top: Bark easily "slips" off at the right time during the growing season.

Opposite Bottom Left: Inserting a chip bud into a host tree trunk.

Opposite Bottom Right: Grafting grapevines is one way to save money if you plan to grow a mini vineyard.

A BIT OF ADVICE

Prep your tape before you begin joining a scion to a host tree. Tear or cut a length of grafting tape from the roll and attach one end to the host tree. When you make your splice or budding cuts, and join the scion or bud to the host, the tape will be ready to use.

Attach grafting tape to the host tree, wrap the graft thoroughly, tie off the tape, and paint with wax if needed.

Opposite: Increase fruit production in small-space gardens with grafting.

START SOMEWHERE

Whether you buy a reliable grafted or multi-fruit tree from a nursery or attempt to create your own at home, just do your research and go for it. Don't let these unfamiliar, advanced space-saving concepts stop you from having the mini fruit garden of your dreams. Remember that not every graft takes, nor does every tree thrive. But it's about the process and learning along the way. Mistakes are learning opportunities, and failures open the door to something new. The excitement of harvesting your first home-grown plum and peach from the same tree is worth the effort.

In the next chapter we'll focus on the techniques for planting your new fruit trees.

Guerrilla Grafting

In cities all over the world, rebel gardeners are grafting fruit tree scions to non-fruiting street trees in an effort to bring fruit to the public. By grafting fruiting plum, cherry, and pear scion wood onto ornamental trees in the same family, grafters unlock the potential of free public fruit everywhere. Visit GuerrillaGrafters.org for more info.

Opposite: Grafted fruit trees will fit in your container gardening.

Container-grown cane berries can be part of your mini fruit garden in addition to fruit trees.

CHAPTER 5
Let's Get Planting!

Congratulations! You've done your research, made a plan, and designed your new mini fruit garden on paper. You've prepped your soil and tested for adequate drainage (go back to "Preparing the Soil" in chapter 2 if you haven't done this). Now you're ready to plant those trees. In this chapter we'll cover the basics both of in-ground and container planting of fruit trees, cane berries, and fruiting shrubs. You'll find individual planting instructions for berries later in chapter 6, so once you feel confident with the basics in this chapter, flip ahead for detailed planting instructions.

IN-GROUND PLANTING

It bears repeating that bed preparation is the most important task before planting a new tree in the ground. Before you begin, make sure your soil is moist but not soggy. Avoid digging waterlogged soils because doing so can damage the soil structure and cause future soil compaction issues. In other words, plant at least a few days after a heavy rainfall or after watering deeply to allow soil to drain before digging the hole.

Gather your tools for planting a tree: shovel, gloves, fruit tree, tarp, and broom handle or stick.

DIGGING THE HOLE

The instinct when planting a tree is to dig a hole only slightly larger than the nursery pot or rootball. Resist this urge. Instead, aim for a saucer-shaped hole that tapers outward toward the edges. Make the saucer hole between 3 to 8 feet [.9 to 2.4 meters] in diameter, depending on the size of the tree. The rule of thumb is two to three times as wide as the rootball. The bottom of the hole should be the same depth as the rootball or slightly shallower. Place any removed soil in a bucket or on a tarp nearby, but do not pile it up around the edges of the planting hole. The reason why will become clear in a minute.

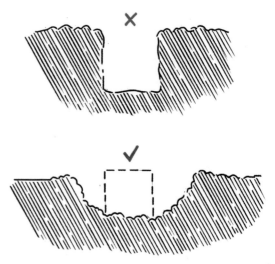

The ideal way to dig a planting hole for your fruit tree is wide and sloping rather than narrow and cylindrical.

IDENTIFYING THE GRAFT UNION AND SOIL LINE

The graft union is located on the trunk where rootstock joins the scion. While most fruit trees are grafted, a rare few, such as fig trees, are not, so they will not have a graft union. The graft union or graft point is often slightly larger than the rest of the trunk or rounded around the middle. Once you have identified the graft point, locate the soil line. The soil line is obvious on potted trees. It is simply the top of the soil level in the nursery pot. Bare-root trees lack soil, of course, so to find the soil line on bare-root trees, look for a change in color along the bark. The darker bark was buried underground and should be located a couple inches above the first root flare. (The root flare is where the trunk branches off into roots and the texture of the bark changes. The first root flare is slightly higher than the other roots.) The graft union and soil line will help you assess the right depth for your tree.

Next, take a broom handle and lay it across the planting hole. This will clearly mark the current soil level of the planting area to keep you from planting the tree too deeply or too shallowly (aren't you glad you piled that extra soil somewhere else?). For potted trees, loosen the rootball on the sides and bottom. Inspect the root system for any circling roots. Loosen or cut them with pruning shears to redirect and encourage roots to grow in a new direction. Don't be afraid to trim long roots. The tree will send out new growth once planted. Gently lower the tree into the planting hole. For bare-root trees, form a cone of soil in the bottom of the planting hole and drape the roots over the cone. Angle the roots down and out.

A broom handle serves as a guide for planting depth.

For bare root stock, trim long roots with shears. For potted trees, break roots apart with your hands.

Trees don't like to be buried too deeply. Locate the first root flare at the top of the rootball to use as a guide for planting depth.

Use a broom handle to align the trunk to the soil level below the graft union.

PLANTING DEPTH

Before you backfill the hole, let's talk about planting depth. Experts disagree on how deep to plant a fruit tree. Some sources suggest planting at the same soil level as the nursery pot or at the soil line on a bare-root tree. Others insist that the first root flare should be slightly exposed after planting. While it's true that fruit trees thrive best if the first root flare is exposed on an established tree, let's meet halfway and plant the tree to a depth somewhere between the soil line and the first root flare. Once the tree is established and sending out new growth, you can dig to expose that first root flare knowing that it won't be buried too deeply.

Align the trunk with the broom handle somewhere between the soil line and the first root flare. The graft union should be above both of these markers. If not, make sure at least the graft union is above the broom handle. Backfill the hole with native soil from your tarp or bucket, and firm the soil slightly around its roots to help keep the tree upright. Water gently with a dilution of kelp emulsion to fill in any air pockets and ease transplant shock. Add more soil as needed.

Opposite: Gently backfill the planting hole with soil. Avoid compressing the soil too much.

A properly staked tree will develop a strong trunk with minimal support.

STAKING

Many fruit trees are sold tethered to a wooden stake. This stake is for stability during its time at the nursery. Once planted, it's time to up the staking game. Bare-root and very dwarf trees may not need staking at all, but larger trees may benefit from the addition of loose support.

In locations where deer and other wildlife tend to nibble on tree bark, consider installing a tree guard to protect young trees. Read more about this and other protections for your new fruit trees in chapter 9.

Nursery stock often comes tied to a stake. Make plans to remove it soon after planting or follow instructions on the next page to stake it properly.

Tough Love Support

The goal of staking is to provide support but not reliance. Your tree will need to develop strength on its own, and if it remains taped to the stake that came with it, the trunk is less likely to thicken and grow stronger. Here is the best way to stake a young tree.

First, remove the stake that came with the tree. Then, install two larger stakes, one on either side of the tree, about 1 foot [30 cm] away from the trunk. Next, wrap a length of rubber tubing threaded with wire around the trunk and connect both ends to one stake. Repeat this process for the other stake. The loops should be loose enough to allow movement so the tree can bend in the wind but not topple. Make sure the wire is covered with tubing where it contacts the tree to prevent damage to the bark or girdling. Once the tree has grown in, these supports won't be needed anymore. This is after a year or so, once the tree has anchored and thickened.

Gather your equipment: rubber tubing, wire, 3-inch [7.5-cm] diameter stakes, and a mallet.

Install two stakes, one on either side of the tree.

Secure tubing to one stake, looping the tree . . .

Then the other.

CONTAINER PLANTING

Once you've prepared your containers for planting (see "Container Prep" sidebar), you're ready to install your young fruit trees in pots. Unlike in-ground planting, container fruit trees require imported soil and amendments. Do not use native soil in containers; it is often too dense for proper drainage. Your local nursery will have bagged soil mixes for all types of plants: potting soil, acidic planting mix, cactus mix, and so forth. There may even be a mix just for fruit trees. The important thing is to make sure the mix has plenty of organic matter and perlite for drainage and air circulation. (If the label doesn't clearly state the ingredients, ask your nursery which mix is best for the type of tree you want to plant.)

While a commercial container potting soil is perfectly sufficient for the job, some fruits require faster-draining or more acidic soil. For example, citrus trees prefer a mix of potting soil and cactus mix or sand to improve drainage. Blueberries prefer a lower soil pH so an acidic planting mix is a must. Ask at your nursery for product guidance based on the trees you plan to grow.

Container Prep

To prepare your containers for planting, empty them of old soil and scrub the inside with a wire brush. This will remove calcifications, hard water deposits, and old soil. Ensure the drainage hole is adequate or drill additional holes if needed. For ceramic or stone pots, use a masonry drill bit, or ask your local nursery if they offer the service. Many do. Rinse the pot well and you're ready to plant. Consider elevating containers with decorative pot feet. They're not only decorative, they increase air circulation and help prevent roots from clogging the pot's drainage hole. Once your containers are clean and situated in their new home, you're ready to move on to the next step.

A well-draining potting soil specifically for containers is your best bet.

Gravel or No Gravel?

Old school experts used to recommend adding broken pottery or a layer of gravel at the bottom of a pot before planting a fruit tree. Not anymore. Turns out, tree roots prefer straight soil instead. If you're worried about losing soil through the drainage hole, you can put a mesh screen over the hole, but it really isn't necessary.

Nix the gravel.

PLANTING POTTED TREES IN CONTAINERS

Fill one-third to one-half of the pot with potting soil depending on the size of your fruit tree's rootball. You can set the potted tree in your container to gauge the soil line and lift it out to add more soil. Mix in a small amount of organic fruit tree fertilizer and a handful or two of worm castings. Then remove the fruit tree from its nursery pot and loosen the roots. Cut away any circling or dead roots, and gently lower the rootball into the pot. Add potting soil to backfill, adding a little more organic fruit tree fertilizer 1 inch [2.5 cm] or so from the top. Fill to the soil line or just below, and water well with diluted kelp emulsion to remove air pockets and ease transplant shock.

Start with one-third potting soil to judge the depth of the rootball; then add more soil as needed.

Check the level of the graft union and first root flare and adjust the soil level at the bottom of the pot as needed. The first root flare should be about 1 inch [2.5 cm] below the lip of the pot.

Make a cone of soil at the bottom for bare-root fruit trees.

PLANTING BARE-ROOT TREES IN CONTAINERS

Fill one-third to one-half of the pot with potting soil and mix in some organic fruit tree fertilizer and a handful or two of worm castings. Form a cone of soil in the center of the pot. Lower the bare-root tree into the pot and drape its roots over the cone. Trim away any roots that are too long, rather than wrapping them around in the pot. Don't worry about cutting roots. The tree will generate new root growth once planted. Gently backfill with soil to cover the roots. Add a little more organic fruit tree fertilizer about 1 inch [2.5 cm] above the buried roots, then fill the pot with soil to the soil line or below. Water well with a diluted kelp emulsion to remove air pockets and ease transplant shock.

As with in-ground planted trees, your new baby might need staking. Most container trees don't require it, but if yours is a bit floppy, follow the instructions under "Staking" to install supports until the tree fills out.

For guidance on planting cane berries, bush berries, and strawberries, turn to chapter 6, but before we move on . . .

Opposite: Gently backfill soil around the rootball.

ONE LAST THING

There you have it. You've planted a fruit tree or berry bush! Pat yourself on the back; you should be proud. There's one last thing to do before we move on. You might not like it, but it is an important step to ensure success.

Remove any existing fruit or flowers from the tree or shrub. *What?!!? But . . . the goal is fruit, right?* Yes, the goal is fruit. Eventually. But first the goal is root development and new leaf growth. Once those are achieved, then you can concentrate on fruit. If you leave fruit and flowers on the tree, all the tree's energy will focus on ripening that fruit. Roots will stay small and future yields will be unimpressive. Instead, sacrifice the fruit and flowers now to promote new growth, deep roots, and higher yields for years to come. Just do it. Really. You won't regret it next year. But before we move on to the care and pruning of fruit trees, let's take a shortcut to explore the world of berries and other fruits that don't grow on trees. The next chapter will cover selection, care, and pruning of strawberries, blueberries, grapes, and more. Once we've covered that topic, then we'll rejoin the path to learn more about fruit tree care.

Explore the possibility of unusual fruits for your mini fruit garden.

CHAPTER 6
Berries and Other Fruits

This chapter is dedicated to growing cane berries, bush or shrub berries, and other fruits that do not grow on trees. This subject has its own chapter because planting, care, and maintenance for berries is different from fruit trees. You will, however, find information on berry diseases in chapter 9 along with fruit trees because some diseases equally target fruits that grow on bushes and vines as well as trees. Berries can be a wonderful addition to small-space gardens, and with a little planning, you can enjoy fresh berries on your morning granola for years to come. Let's delve into the typical behavior and needs of berries.

Much like stone fruits, berries are available in early-, mid-, and late-season varieties. When choosing cane berries, you can grow blackberries, raspberries, golden raspberries, black raspberries (native wild raspberries), boysenberries, loganberries, and olallieberries (the last two named are both blackberry-raspberry hybrids) in either thorny or thornless options. Shrub berries such as blueberries, gooseberries, and currants offer a more compact option without the need for trellising or protection against runners. Strawberries provide groundcover and can be tucked into small spaces or grown vertically. Depending on the amount of space and time you want to commit to these tempting fruits, an abundance of options awaits you. Different regions are better suited to one cultivar over another. Your local agricultural Extension office will have a list of ideal cultivars for your climate.

Berries tend to produce over a short period of time, from a few weeks to a month or so. That's why it's a good idea, if you have room, to choose one each of an early, midseason, and late-season variety to extend your growing season. After all, there is only so much jam and pie one can make with a fresh harvest.

Better to spread the harvest out over spring, summer, and fall if you can. Since agricultural research usually caters to farmers and researchers, its guidance for early-, mid-, and late-season varieties will be useful in determining which cultivars to choose for your mini fruit garden.

GROWING CANE BERRIES

Cane berries include blackberries, raspberries, boysenberries, loganberries, and other brambles. There is one important thing you need to know about this family of plants: brambles are runners! The roots spread out to seek water and send up runners (baby brambles) where you least expect. Take steps to contain the mother plant early on, lest you find yourself digging out runners everywhere—*everywhere*—for the rest of your life. Even if you plant a blackberry in a container on soil, it will grow through the drainage hole and set up shop, running outward up to 15 feet [4.6 meters] away. How to keep them in check? You can put a saucer under the pot to keep them from running or elevate the pot on "pot feet" to allow roots to air prune.

When planting in the ground, seriously consider installing a 2- to 3-foot-deep [.6- to .9-meter-deep] root barrier around a plant at planting time if you don't have room to let them roam. Root barriers are available at nurseries, irrigation supply stores, and hardware stores. They are designed to prevent tree roots from growing under sidewalks and streets. Dig a circular trench (or half-moon if it's against a wall) several feet away from the planting hole, install the root barrier, and rest easy that your brambles will stay contained within that space.

Brambles are somewhat challenging to work with because of their thorny nature. Hybrid thornless varieties solve that problem while providing delicious berries. A pair of thick gloves and long sleeves will make interacting with your cane berries much easier if you do choose varieties with thorns. Here are the specifics for plant spacing and more:

Plant spacing: 3 to 4 feet [.9 to 1.2 meters] apart for blackberries, 2 to 3 feet [.6 to .9 meters] apart for raspberries

Plants per person: ½ to 1

Sunlight: full sun to partial shade—6 to 8 hours of direct sunlight (but reflective light works too)

Ideal container specs: at least 15 inches [38 cm] deep, 15 inches [38 cm] in diameter, good drainage, slightly elevated or on a saucer

Additional requirements: Trellising or guide wires for upright varieties. For in-ground plantings, use T-posts placed 5 to 8 feet [1.5 to 2.4 meters] apart with wire that runs along the front edge of your cane berry patch if growing against a wall. If growing in an open garden space, create a border on both sides of each row of plants with wire connected to the outer edges of each T-post. That will keep the canes contained within the wire supports. Trellising is not required for trailing varieties, unless you want to grow them in an upright fashion in small spaces.

Fruiting Period: Spring in warm-winter climates; summer and early fall in colder climates

Root barriers are lifesavers when it comes to growing cane berries.

Cane berries are worth the effort once you taste their homegrown sweetness.

PRIMOCANES AND FLORICANES

Cane berries grow and fruit on either first- or second-year growth, depending on the variety. First-year canes are called "primocanes" and second-year canes are called "floricanes." Blackberries typically grow new vegetative canes in the first year (primocanes), then those canes fruit the next year (they become floricanes). While those floricanes are fruiting, new primocanes are growing from the soil and will become next year's fruiting canes. Primocanes are green with vigorous young leaves. Floricanes produce fruit clusters, darken as they age, and die completely at the end of the season. Floricanes also generate side branches that can grow 8 to 10 feet [2.4 to 3 meters] long if allowed.

To confuse the situation a smidge, some blackberry and raspberry varieties produce fruit both on primocanes *and* floricanes. Primocanes on fall raspberries, for example, will produce a crop in fall, then again the following year before dying off. Details about the varieties you choose will aid in knowing how to prune them when the time comes (we'll cover this in chapter 8).

UPRIGHT VS. TRAILING

Depending on the variety you choose, your cane berries will grow in an upright or trailing habit. Upright varieties grow 4 to 5 feet [1.2 to 1.5 meters] tall, and longer canes begin to bow over and elongate as the season progresses. Allow enough wall space for upright varieties or use guideposts and wires on both sides if they are growing in the middle of a garden area.

Trailing varieties have less of a running habit, but existing canes may root and propagate if allowed to touch the ground. Create a berry batch for trailing varieties with clearly defined pathways between plants for easy harvesting. In small spaces, tie up trailing canes to guide wires as with upright varieties.

Blackberries darken and soften as they become ripe. They should separate easily from the cane when they're ready to pick.

PLANTING CANE BERRIES

Blackberries, raspberries, boysenberries, loganberries, and other brambles are fairly indestructible. You can take a runner from an existing mother plant, with a root or two, and simply plant it in soil. The canes will die back, but the roots are perennial and will send up new canes in no time. Brambles don't require rich soil but they do need good drainage. They also prefer a soil pH between 6.0 to 7.0. While cane berries prefer full sun, they will tolerate some shade. If you have a spot that doesn't get full sun, try planting a bramble there. With reflective light from neighboring buildings, they will still produce fruit.

Plant cane berries in late winter or early spring from either bare-root or potted nursery stock. Place plants 3 to 5 feet [.9 to 1.5 meters] apart for blackberries, 2 to 3 feet [.6 to .9 meters] apart for raspberries. Soil should be well draining and loose, not soggy or compacted. Amend with compost to open

Diluted kelp emulsion helps ease transplant shock.

compacted soil structures and increase soil fertility but hold off on adding fertilizer until four to six weeks after planting. Dig a hole the same depth or slightly shorter than the nursery pot. Remove the plant from the nursery pot and inspect the rootball for circling roots. Loosen the rootball before lowering it into the planting hole. Hold the rootball in place as you backfill soil around the roots. Make sure to cover any young sprouts at the base of the plant. Gently firm the soil and water well to remove any air pockets.

If you're planting a bare-root cane berry, remove the plant from the sawdust or moist material it arrived in and soak the roots in water for an hour before planting. Dig a hole as deep and wide as the bulk of the root mass. Form a cone of soil in the base of the planting hole and drape the roots over the cone in all directions. If necessary, trim back long roots rather than wrapping them around in the planting hole. Gently backfill soil over the roots and firm the soil. Water well to remove air pockets.

The next step with bare-root planting is to cut back the tops of the canes. Trim back canes to about 4 inches [10 cm] above soil level. This will focus the plants energy on root production. Don't worry; new canes will spring forth from the soil in no time.

FEEDING AND HARVESTING CANE BERRIES

BLACKBERRIES

Once established, blackberries are not heavy feeders. In-ground older plants may not require fertilizing at all in rich, loamy soil. In the first two years, however, young plants benefit from feeding as buds begin to leaf out and again after harvest is finished. Feed container-grown berries as you would young plants, since nutrients will flush out and will need to be replenished over time. As described, fertilize blackberries for the first time four to six weeks after planting. Use a balanced organic all-purpose fertilizer and apply according to package directions. In successive years, you may need to increase the amount of fertilizer per plant. Spread fertilizer in a circle around the canes starting 4 inches [10 cm] away from the cluster of canes, out to 2 feet [.6 meters].

Harvest blackberries when they darken to black with no trace of red. Blackberries that are ripe will come off the bramble into your hand without resistance. Blackberries still tinged with red will be tart and firm. When they are ripe, they will give slightly to the touch. Hold the berry between your thumb and forefinger and gently rock the berry toward and away from you. If it resists at all, leave it for another day. Store unwashed berries in a glass container in the refrigerator and wash before eating. You can freeze blackberries in a single layer on a baking sheet for an hour, then transfer them to a plastic freezer bag for longer storage. Use them in smoothies, make ice cream or sorbet, or process them for jam.

Ripe cane berries separate easily from their canes; there's no need to force it.

RASPBERRIES

Raspberries, similar to blackberries, don't want fertilizer at planting time. Wait to fertilize until about six weeks after planting. Use an organic berry fertilizer or one for acid-loving plants, with higher levels of nitrogen and phosphorus. Avoid too much nitrogen, which will trigger ample leafy growth but no fruit. Mix it with a little compost and spread it around each plant. The general rule of thumb is to apply fertilizer in winter or early spring, before fruit sets, but avoid applying fertilizer after midsummer.

The technique for harvesting raspberries is like that of blackberries. Use your thumb and forefinger to gently rock the fruit toward and away from you. If it comes off easily, it is ready. If it resists, it's not. See the "Raspberry and Blackberry ID" sidebar for distinguishing characteristics. Raspberries should give slightly to the touch when they're ripe. If they are firm, leave them on the vine another day or so and test again. Store unwashed berries in a glass container in the refrigerator and wash before eating. You can freeze them in a single layer on a baking sheet for an hour, then transfer them to a plastic freezer bag for longer storage.

OTHER CANE BERRIES

The general guideline for feeding cane berry crosses and hybrids such as boysenberries, marionberries, and black raspberries is to fertilize them in early spring at budbreak and again as flowers are beginning to open. Fertilize every four weeks but only if needed; many cane berries grow sufficiently without additional fertilizer. Test your soil for nutrient levels, apply compost and worm castings, and see how it goes. Adjust your feeding schedule based on your soil's needs and take note of what worked and what didn't.

Raspberry and Blackberry ID

How to know your blackberries from your raspberries? Blackberries take the receptacle, or core, of the berry with it when harvested, but raspberries will leave the receptacle behind on the vine. Thus, raspberries will be hollow inside, but blackberries won't be.

Boysenberries (or loganberries) keep things interesting in the garden.

Dead canes are easy to spot. They are brown and brittle at the end of the season.

PRUNING CANE BERRIES

Taming these monsters require extra layers of clothing and thick gloves to wrestle prickly, long canes back into bounds each year. In wild spaces, homeowners sometimes hire goats to eat the canes down to nubbins, but in your mini fruit garden a goat might be overkill. Here are a few guidelines for pruning cane berries.

Pruning is best done at the end of the season in late fall or early winter once fruit-producing canes have died back. If canes don't die back completely by winter where you live, mark the canes that produced fruit with clothespins or twine during the growing season so you'll know which canes to cut down. Follow these steps:

1. Using long-handled loppers, cut all upright and trailing canes back to 4 feet [1.2 meters] tall or long, just above an outward-facing bud. (See chapter 8 under "Two Kinds of Cuts" to identify where to make the cut.)

2. Cut any brown and dead canes down to soil level.
3. Remove any lateral or horizontal crossing branches growing off the main canes, cutting back to one or two buds.
4. For blackberries: Remove thin or spindly older canes at soil level. For raspberries: Reduce the number of canes to five or six of the strongest canes per plant. Avoid removing new canes, which are usually bright green, since those will be the fruit-producing floricanes next year.

If you are anchoring any runners for new plants, check to see if they have established strong roots. If they have, then cut the cane from the mother plant and train accordingly.

The pruning process can take time so don't be afraid to break up the task into steps. Tackle step one on day one, then steps two through four on day two. Before long, your cane berries will be ready for spring and order will be restored.

GROWING BLUEBERRIES AND OTHER BUSH BERRIES

Blueberries, gooseberries, and currants are on the list of the plentiful bush or shrub berries that you can grow in your mini fruit garden. Many lend themselves well to growing in containers, and they maintain a smaller footprint than cane berries so they are perfect for small spaces. While gooseberries and currants mainly grow in cool regions, blueberries and some gooseberries have been bred for low-chill environments.

Bush berries have an upright growth habit and can tolerate partial shade. They all require adequate moisture and acidic soil. Bush berries do best when planted in fall. Many are considered self-fertile, but they fruit more abundantly with a pollinizer close by. Plant different varieties together to ensure adequate pollination.

Plant spacing: 4 to 5 feet [1.2 to 1.5 meters] apart

Plants per person: 1 to 2

Sunlight: full sun to partial shade for blueberries and currants; morning sun and afternoon shade for gooseberries

Ideal container specs: at least 18 inches [45 cm] deep, 20 inches [50 cm] in diameter, good drainage

Additional requirements: acidic soil amendments for both in-ground and containers

Fruiting period: spring in warm regions, summer in cold-winter regions

HIGHBUSH AND LOWBUSH BLUEBERRIES

Let's focus on blueberries for a moment. Blueberries are available in highbush and lowbush varieties. Highbush types are most commonly grown in warmer climates, coastal areas, and even in some cooler territories (low-chill varieties are available for warm and coastal areas and are usually labeled as Southern highbush). They grow between 6 to 8 feet [1.8 to 2.4 meters] tall.

Lowbush varieties are grown in colder locations with harsh temperatures. Lowbush types are perfect for enduring freezing winters, mainly because they are short. They tolerate a thick blanket of snow without suffering damage. The snow insulates them over winter, and they leaf out in spring, defiant as ever. Another category, half-highbush, is mainly comprised of hybrids that grow to a height between low- and highbush types and tolerate colder temperatures.

CHOOSING VARIETIES

As mentioned in chapter 3, chill hours is an important consideration when choosing the right variety for your mini fruit garden. Pair that criterion with the ideal highbush or lowbush type for your growing area and dedicate space for at least two plants (e.g., 'Sharpblue' and 'O'Neal') to pollinate each other, and you're on your way.

Opposite Top: Blueberries are satisfying to grow at home. Plant two different varieties to ensure a bountiful crop.

Opposite Bottom: Blueberries make beautiful landscape plants while flowering and fruiting.

PLANTING BUSH BERRIES

Bush or shrub berries have an upright growth behavior without runners and are therefore much more compliant when asked to stay within boundaries. They grow well in containers or in the ground, although some require more acidic soil than others. Some have spines, others don't.

Shrub berries require acidic soil. Blueberries prefer a soil pH below 5.2, so consider planting them in containers filled with acidic planting mix or adding sulphur to existing soil if it is very alkaline. Gooseberries and currants can tolerate soils with a pH between 5.5 to 7.0. See the "Blueberries Need Acidic Soil" sidebar for details on how to lower the soil pH naturally both in-ground and in container-planted blueberries. Plant shrub berries 3 to 5 feet [.9 to 1.5 meters] apart in well-drained, nutrient-rich soil. Amend the soil with plenty of compost or rotted manure and mix in a handful of organic berry fertilizer if needed.

The best time to plant bare-root or potted nursery stock is fall to early spring. In locations where winter is frosty, dig the hole in fall, but plant in spring. Prepare the planting hole as deep as the nursery pot or slightly deeper for currents and gooseberries. For those crops, plan to cover the lower stems with soil to a depth of two or three buds to encourage root development. Plant blueberries at soil level.

Remove the plant from the pot and inspect the roots for circling. Loosen the rootball before lowering it into the planting hole. Gently backfill around the rootball and firm the soil. Water to remove air pockets.

When planting a bare-root shrub berry, remove the plant from the sawdust or moist material it arrived in and soak the roots in water for several hours before planting. Dig a hole as deep and wide as the bulk of the root mass. Form a cone of soil in the base of the planting hole and drape the roots over the cone in all directions. If necessary, trim back long roots rather than wrapping them around in the planting hole. Gently backfill soil over the roots and firm the soil. Water well to remove air pockets.

If planting currants and gooseberries in spring, tip prune branches back to the fifth bud up from soil level. Water well to remove air pockets. As with fruit trees, remove any fruit or flowers forming at planting time to force the plants' energy to focus on root production instead of fruit production. Once established you will be rewarded with an abundant harvest. Add a layer of mulch around plants to help retain moisture and keep roots cool.

FEEDING AND HARVESTING SHRUB AND OTHER BERRIES

BLUEBERRIES

As with cane berries, wait to fertilize blueberries until four weeks after planting, and again in late spring. They generally require only one or two applications of fertilizer per season, unless planted in sandy soil or containers. Apply an organic berry fertilizer specifically for acid-loving plants around the base of each plant, 4 inches [10 cm] away from the trunk out to the drip line. In soils with low organic matter, feed plants every six weeks through the season, stopping at midsummer. Fertilizer quantities differ for young plants vs. older counterparts. Start with the lowest amount recommended. In the coming years, you will increase the amount of fertilizer given to each plant to support larger growth and higher fruit production. See the "Blueberries Need Acidic Soil" sidebar for instructions on watering with vinegar to lower soil pH throughout the season.

Opposite: Garden-fresh fruits are worth the work.

To harvest blueberries, observe the color to know when they are ripe. Avoid picking berries with traces of red or green on ripe berries. Instead, look for dark blue or pink, depending on the variety. Look for a dusty film on the fruit and inspect near the stem end for any traces of red. Berry surfaces without sun exposure will ripen last, so check those undersides for color. Some varieties may display a red ring around the stem end if they are not ripe. That ring will disappear once ripe. Ripening is usually complete within a week or two of the color changing to blue.

Like cane berries, blueberries should come away from the stem easily when ready to harvest. If the fruit doesn't come off easily with light pressure, leave it for another day or two. Conversely, if you prefer your berries tart or want to gather them before the birds do, pick them a little early and increase the sweetener in your recipe when processing them. Store berries in glass containers with a dry paper towel on the bottom to absorb moisture. They will last about a week in the fridge.

GOOSEBERRIES AND CURRANTS

Gooseberries and currants are considered heavy feeders and, as mentioned, they prefer their soil mixed with extra compost or aged manure before planting. Both grow best with sufficient amounts of phosphorus and potassium in the soil, with gooseberries requiring less nitrogen than currants. Feed them a mixture of organic berry fertilizer for acid-loving plants and compost in early spring, starting 4 inches [10 cm] away from the base of the plant out to a 2-foot [60-cm] diameter. Because of their relatively shallow root systems, they also benefit from a thick layer of mulch to keep roots cool and happy. Remember, mulch is a fungal food so it helps improve soil microbial activity as well.

Most gooseberries and currants will start to produce fruit a year or two after planting, increasing in production each year. Both are similar to citrus in that they can live on the bush while ripe and don't require immediate picking. Don your long sleeves and gloves for harvesting gooseberries as they produce a sharp

Blueberries Need Acidic Soil

In addition to proper nutrients to encourage flowering and fruiting, blueberries need soil that has a pH between 4.3 to 5.5. Sometimes a foundation of acid planting mix isn't enough. Use this trick from the folks at Two Dog Organic Nursery in Los Angeles, CA, USA: acidify your soil by watering with distilled vinegar every two months. Add 4 tablespoons [60 ml] vinegar to 2 gallons [7.8 liters] water and drench each plant. Your blueberries will reward you with a bountiful harvest.

Apple cider vinegar helps lower the soil pH for blueberries.

Opposite: Bush berries round out your fruit garden with color and fresh flavor.

thorn or tail on the bottom of each berry. The thorns can be left on during harvest to keep them fresh but remove them before eating. Gooseberries come off easily when ripe. If you plan to bake gooseberries into a pie, you can pick them when fully formed but green. For fresh eating, wait until they are fully ripe before picking. Harvest individual gooseberries and store in a glass container in the refrigerator for up to three days.

Currants are ready to pick when they are richly colored and soft. Because of their delicate state during harvesting, use pruning shears to clip clusters rather than individual fruits. You can also pinch stems with your fingers instead of using shears. Currants can be dried like raisins, made into jam, or stored for fresh eating for about two weeks.

PRUNING BUSH BERRIES

Pruning is an important task to maintain productive plants. If left unchecked, leggy plants develop weak stems that don't properly support their fruit. The best time to prune is while a berry bush is dormant, which is over winter or in early spring before bud-break. Pruning instruction differs depending on the fruit and its growing habits. Some produce on new wood, or older spurs, so it's important to research your specific variety for pruning techniques prior to wielding a blade. Begin by following "The Three Ds" in chapter 8 removing dead, diseased, damaged or disorderly canes and crossing branches. Then find out the fruiting behavior of your particular variety and delve deeper into pruning specifics for those varieties.

As a general rule, blueberries may not need severe pruning in the first few years but benefit from reduction cuts to encourage new growth (see chapter 8 under "Two Kinds of Cuts"). They produce fruit on one-year-old wood so new growth is critical to future productivity. Gooseberries and currants, on the other hand, produce on wood that's two to four years old. Remove older wood and prune back the rest to the best six shoots.

Blueberry leaves turn reddish and drop as the dormant season approaches, which is a signal that soon it will be time to prune.

Opposite: Fresh-picked strawberries are a delightful treat.

GROWING STRAWBERRIES

Homegrown strawberries are a satisfying crop to include in your mini fruit garden. They can be grown in-ground, in containers, or in raised beds. They lend themselves to growing in vertical gardens as well, because the fruit drapes over the edges and stays clear of many pests that regularly hunt for berries laying directly on soil surfaces. Your strawberry patch will range in size, depending on the space available, but here are the guidelines for growing enough for your household.

Plant spacing: 1 foot (30 cm) apart

Plants per person: 6

Sunlight: full sun to partial shade—at least 6 hours of direct sunlight

Ideal container specs: at least 10 inches [25.5 cm] deep, diameter enough for at least 6 plants, good drainage

Fruiting period: Everbearing produce year-round in warm-winter climates; they produce in spring/summer/fall elsewhere. June-bearing produce in late-spring to early-summer

Strawberries grow well in raised beds and other containers.

CHOOSING VARIETIES

Strawberries are sold as either bare-root crowns or potted seedlings. Bare-root options offer a wider selection of varieties. Gardeners can order bare-root crowns online or through seed catalogs in fall for delivery in winter or early spring. Crowns are shipped dormant and you plant them out upon receipt. Dormant crowns usually look sad and almost dead, but don't worry. When you plant them, they will leaf out within a few days to a week. Strawberry seedlings in 4-inch [10-cm] pots or six-packs are available at nurseries, and the selection is usually limited to popular varieties. But before we talk about cultivars, first let's look at the types available and determine which is best for you.

JUNE-BEARING AND EVERBEARING

If you want to make jam or preserves, plant June-bearing strawberry varieties in your garden. They produce a larger crop within a limited time frame over the season (usually harvest lasts two to three weeks), which is perfect timing for preserving. You'll need a lot of strawberries all at once, so June-bearing is your best option.

Everbearing strawberries produce smaller crops several times per season. If you want strawberries for fresh eating over a longer period of time, opt either for everbearing or day neutral types (see the following paragraph). Fruiting times differ, depending on where you live. In warm-winter climates, you can expect a crop of everbearing strawberries as early as late winter, midseason as summer comes on, and again in fall. In cold-winter climates, everbearing strawberries produce a crop in spring, summer, and fall.

You may see sources that talk about day neutral varieties. The term "day neutral" means these varieties don't require a specific day-length in order to fruit so they will produce continuously in most climates. The thing is, most nurseries don't label strawberries as day neutral. You'll see either June-bearing or ever-bearing. It's confusing, but just know that there are day neutral varieties that are labeled as everbearing, such as 'Seascape', and they will produce during the entire season. There are some hybrids, such as 'Sequoia', that are conflictingly labeled as ever-bearing in one catalog and June-bearing in another. So let's not get hung up on these details. Do your research and select the variety that best suits your climate, day length, and needs.

There is a third classification of strawberry to consider for your mini fruit garden. Alpine or wild strawberries produce smaller fruits than typical varieties, but their sugars are concentrated for a burst of sweetness in every bite. Often referred to by their French name of *fraise des bois*, they are a woodland strawberry that grows well in landscapes as a ground-cover and in raised beds. They do not have a running behavior, so they will stay within bounds in tiny gardens. If you want to plant something completely different, choose a white variety. Its white flesh has red seeds when the berries are ripe.

PLANTING STRAWBERRIES

Strawberry plant anatomy consists of the roots, the crown, leaves, fruit, and runners (also called daughters). When planting strawberries, either bare-root or nursery seedlings, the crown is the most important part. The crown is the part of the plant where the roots join the stems and leaves. The crown is usually a darker color than the roots, with no trace of green like the stems. Why is it so important to identify this segment of the plant? If you bury the crown too deeply, then your plant will rot and die. If you leave the crown too exposed above the soil level, it will dry out and wither into oblivion. Channel your inner Goldilocks and plant the crown "just right." Just right is this: bury the roots but leave the crown sitting above soil level.

Strawberries need well-amended soil so add plenty of compost and worm castings before planting. Mix in organic berry fertilizer in the planting hole, and water with kelp emulsion to settle the soil and help reduce transplant shock.

Make sure the crown is above soil level, but not too high, so it's just right!

TO MULCH OR NOT TO MULCH

Mulch is essential for a healthy garden. Chip bark helps keep roots cool, feeds soil microbes, and helps soil retain moisture. But is it always a good idea? When it comes to strawberries, perhaps not. Two of strawberry's main pests are the sow bug (*Oniscidea*) and pill bug (*Armadillidiidae*). These critters love to feed on decaying matter, and while they are there, they nibble on your sweet, hard-earned strawberries too. For this reason, it is important to remove spent foliage around strawberry plants throughout the season. Because mulch is also decaying matter, it can create the perfect environment for sow/pill bugs to populate. You can decide for yourself whether chip bark works in your strawberry patch or not. There are alternatives, such as plastic sheeting or weed barriers. But some consider those unsightly or don't want plastic in their garden. The good news is, when planting bio-intensively, strawberries and other crops will form their own living mulch when they are planted closer together. Eventually the plants and daughters (if they're allowed to root) fill in the space and mulch isn't needed.

FEEDING AND HARVESTING STRAWBERRIES

Strawberries are considered heavy feeders. As with other fruit-producing crops, remove the first set of flowers after planting to focus the plants' energy on root development. After that, feed your strawberry plants as they begin to flower and set fruit. Apply an organic berry fertilizer once per month after testing for nutrient levels in your soil. Remember: Sandy soils will require more frequent addition of nutrients than clay soils. Adjust the feeding schedule based on test results.

Strawberries can develop problems or deformities if certain nutrients or micronutrients are lacking. Cat-facing, for example, is a result of poor pollination or a boron deficiency. Leaves will often turn brown along the edges if the soil is lacking either nitrogen or magnesium. If you are regularly feeding your strawberries and they still show signs of leaf deterioration or deficiency, consider reducing the number of plants in the container or remove all daughter plants.

Cat-facing deforms strawberries, but they are still edible.

Opposite Top: Elevated planters can keep strawberries out of harm's way.

Opposite Bottom: Use your harvest in breakfast each morning or as a midday snack.

To harvest strawberries, look for an even coverage of deep red color. Strawberries are not ripe if there is still a white ring around the stem end of the berry. Look under the calyx, the pointy foliage that tops each berry, to check for ripeness. Wait for the color to change completely before harvesting for the sweetest results. Pinch the stems or snip berries off with shears, keeping some of the stem intact. Store unwashed berries in a glass container with a dry paper towel on the bottom and wash before eating. You can process strawberries into jam, chop and freeze them for smoothies, and bake them into pies.

Read up on strawberry pest and disease issues in chapter 9.

Turn garden harvests into jams and jellies for use later in the year.

PRUNING STRAWBERRIES

Strawberry plants require minimal but important upkeep during and after their season. As mentioned, the most common critters that attack strawberries love decaying matter. Sow bugs and pill bugs make a home under the thick debris of old strawberry leaves so it's critical to remove spent leaves regularly. As leaves yellow, snip stems off at the base of the plant and toss them in your compost bin. Cut off any brown leaves at the base of the plant too. Cut rather than pull, as sometimes pulling will unearth an entire plant.

Inspect the plants for daughters every few weeks and decide whether you want to keep or remove them. There are two schools of thought around daughters. Some gardeners prefer not to keep them because they siphon energy and nutrients away from the mother plant. Other gardeners encourage daughters in order to increase the size of their berry patch by propagating new plants for free. It's up to you. If you plan to keep them, find an open space and pin the daughter vine to the soil to help it develop roots. Once the roots have developed (there should be slight resistance when you gently tug on the plant), "cut the cord" from the mother plant and

Revitalizing Strawberry Plants

Rather than throw away your strawberry plants after a couple of years, you can rejuvenate both plants and soil with this trick: in early spring, before the plants begin flowering, dig up each strawberry plant, including the entire rootball and some soil around it, and set it aside on a tarp or in a box. Next, add a 1- to 2-inch [2.5- to 5-cm] layer of compost to the existing soil and scratch it in with your fingers. Apply organic fruit and berry fertilizer and work it in to the soil. Then replant your strawberry plants 1 foot [30 cm] apart. If you have extras, give them away to fellow gardeners. Water your transplanted strawberry plants with diluted kelp emulsion to ease transplant shock and encourage root development. The strawberries will take root quickly in the richly amended soil and will start producing new leaves and fruit in no time.

trim away the extra length. If you don't want to allow daughters to grow, be diligent about cutting them off at the base of the mother plant.

Even though they are perennial, as strawberry plants age they become less productive. Some gardeners tear out their strawberry patch every two to three years to replace them with fresh plants. See the "Revitalizing Strawberry Plants" sidebar for a trick to save some money and still have high-yielding plants.

GROWING OTHER FRUITS

Now it's time to explore the myriad other fruits that don't grow on trees and bushes. Some are more exotic than others and grow well in warm-winter locations. But with a little effort, they can be grown in greenhouses or near protected sunny walls. If you can't grow these crops in your neck of the woods, don't despair. You can read about and appreciate how to grow them. And maybe someday you'll live in a place where these fruits grow easily. And hardiness zones are shifting. In another decade, you may be able to grow something exotic where you live.

Dragon fruit is a cactus that produces delicious bright pink fruits. Grow it vertically in your mini fruit garden.

DRAGON FRUIT

When gardeners think of fruit, they don't often think of cactus. But that is exactly where dragon fruit comes from. This exotic orb is aptly named for its whimsical scale-patterned exterior, with bright fuchsia or white flesh speckled with black seeds. Also known as pitaya or pitahaya, dragon fruit hails from Central America. It is hardy to 32°F [0°C] but prefers to grow in temperatures between 65°F to 77°F [18°C to 25°C].

Plant spacing: 15 to 25 feet [4.5 to 7.6 meters] apart

Plants per person: 1 plant (1 plant can produce up to 220 pounds [100 kg] of fruit after 4 years)

Sunlight: full sun but protect with shade cloth during first 4 months of growth to prevent sunburn

Ideal container specs: at least 15 inches [37.5 cm] deep, 12 inches [30 cm] in diameter, good drainage

Additional requirements: trellising for wall support or a T-post for stand-alone growing. Dragon fruit is a vigorous grower so trellises must be able to support heavy growth.

Fruiting period: summer through fall in warm-winter climates

Dragon fruit blossoms are exotic and beautiful.

GROWING DRAGON FRUIT

Dragon fruit variety names are some of the more creative in horticulture. From *Hylocereus undatus* 'David Bowie' to *Hylocereus polyrhizus* 'Voodoo Child', there are plenty to choose from. There are even yellow-skinned varieties (*Selenicereus megalanthus*) with white flesh. The black seeds are reminiscent of those found inside kiwi fruit. Some dragon fruits require hand pollination or need to be planted near a pollinizer, but many are self-pollinating or will fruit without hand pollination. Choose a sunny location and determine whether you will grow in-ground or in a container. Make sure to install a very sturdy trellis before planting your dragon fruit. It will need reliable support once it begins to grow.

Traditionally, dragon fruit is guided and tied up a freestanding 4- by 4-foot [1.2- by 1.2-meter] post that is 5 to 6 feet [1.5 to 1.8 meters] tall and draped over crossing horizontal posts at the top. Some clever gardeners build an open frame around those horizontal cross pieces to provide additional support. This allows more growth and harvesting from all sides. With this type of growing situation, you can achieve the aforementioned 220 lb. [100 kg] harvest. Folks who don't have space for a freestanding trellis can use a wall support combined with careful pruning. The harvest may be less, but who needs that much fruit, anyway?

PLANTING DRAGON FRUIT

Dragon fruit grows easily from cuttings, which is great if you have a friend who is already growing dragon fruit. This cactus grows in segments that widen and narrow as new segments develop. As with most cactus and succulents, simply cut a segment from an existing plant (always ask permission before taking cuttings from someone else's plants, okay?). Ideally, choose segments that are at least 8 inches [20 cm] long. Shorter segments can take longer to sprout roots and new growth. Also, pay attention to which way is up. You'll need to remember this

for later when planting the cutting. FYI—the spines point diagonally up and out. If you clip a segment at a narrow point, you can plant that narrow tip several inches deep in soil. For greater success, however, cut another 2 to 3 inches [5 to 7.5 cm] off the bottom on the diagonal, and place the cuttings in a dry, indoor location out of direct sunlight for three days to cure over the cut end. Next, prepare your soil.

Cacti prefer sandy, well-draining soil, but dragon fruit want more nutrients than most cacti need. To accommodate this, incorporate some organic matter into a sandy potting mix if you're growing them in a container, and amend existing in-ground soil with plenty of compost and sand to ensure it drains well. Dragon fruit also need water; just because it's a cactus doesn't mean it can go without water. Think of dragon fruit as a tropical fruit that likes rain and more regular moisture. In containers, water dragon fruit once per week in dry climates. Let the soil dry out between waterings for in-ground plantings.

FEEDING AND HARVESTING DRAGON FRUIT

As mentioned, dragon fruit require richer soil and more nutrients than do most cacti. Feed your plants growing in containers, a month or two after they begin to grow new segments, with a balanced organic fertilizer that has between 4 to 8 percent phosphorus and potassium. Continue to feed every other month during the growing season. Aged manure can be applied in the first year around, but not touching, the plants. As it grows you will increase the amounts of organic fertilizer and manure around each plant during the growing season.

It may take a year or two before dragon fruit begin to flower and set fruit. When they do, it's a beautiful thing. The flowers are otherworldly white blossoms with pale yellow centers that spring from the sides of the cactus. To hand-pollinate a dragon fruit, get out a paintbrush and a flashlight. That's right; the flowers open in the evening, so that's the best time to pollinate. Wear a headlamp to keep your hands free

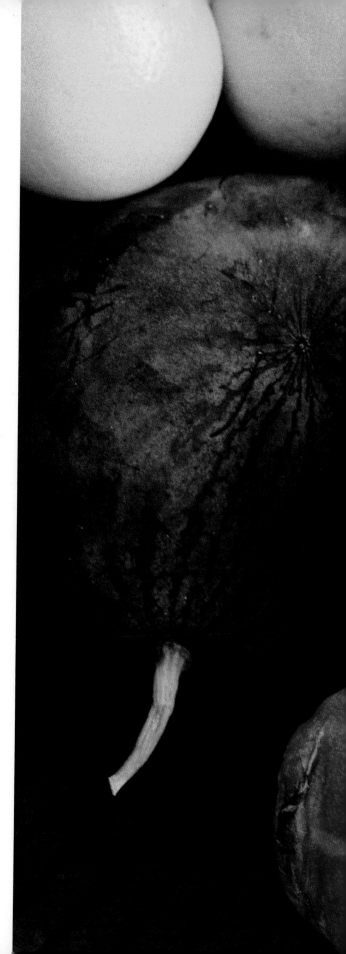

and head out to your garden after dark. Pollen will be located inside the base of the flower surrounding and beneath the yellow anthers. Pollen often drops onto the petals below the anthers or sits at the base inside the flower. The stigma, the female part of a flower, will extend outward from that base on its own stem. Ideally, paint the pollen from one flower onto the stigma of a different flower to ensure cross-pollination. If only one flower is in bloom, paint loose pollen from the (male) anthers to the extended stigma.

To harvest dragon fruit, look for a few signs. First, the color will turn from green to pink/red or yellow, depending on the variety you've chosen. The color should be even and bright across the entire surface. The scales on the fruit, or "wings" as they are often called, will become brownish and begin to wither or dry. Last, the fruit should give slightly when you squeeze it. If it is firm, wait another day or so and check again. It is important to know that dragon fruit does not ripen once picked so keep an eye out for ripe fruit. If the fruit looks blotchy or shriveled it is most likely overripe. Typically, it takes about four days to ripen once the fruit turns color.

Now put on your gloves, the kind you'd wear when working with roses. You know, heavy-duty, thorn-resistant gloves. While the pink cultivars don't have thorns on the fruits themselves, yellow dragon fruits do. Remove the thorns with pliers before or after harvesting the yellow type fruits. You can also wear those thick gloves and brush the thorns off in a downward motion away from you. For the red/pink varieties, you will want to wear gloves to protect against the cactus as you harvest the fruit. Dragon fruit comes off the plant with a twist or two. If it doesn't twist off easily, it isn't ready to pick. Wait a day or two and check again.

Opposite: Bright pink flesh makes dragon fruit appealing and delicious.

Twist or use shears to harvest dragon fruit.

PRUNING DRAGON FRUIT

Dragon fruit may require pruning up to three times per year in order to keep it in-bounds. Tendrils will form on the cactus to grab on to supports such as trellises and walls. Use wire that has been threaded through an old hose or similar tubing to prevent damage to the cactus as you tie it to the trellis or post. If you are using the traditional post-type trellising method, the segments will grow to the top and eventually curve outward and down away from the center post. It will look like a water fountain when it's fully grown—a prickly but beautiful water fountain. If you are growing up a wall or flat trellis, your job is to keep the plant growing upward to the top of the trellis. You can allow some segments to arch downward once they reach the top if you secure those segments to the trellis. Use clean pruning shears to cut away (and give away) segments that grow outward from the trellis or support post if they fall out of bounds.

GRAPES

Grapes evoke romantic notions of ancient festivals, French vineyards, and *terroir*. They are a perennial crop that fruit on climbing vines, available as seedless or seeded table grapes for eating (and drying into raisins) or as more hardy varieties for making your own wine. Some growers use dry farming methods while others keep them well irrigated. While winemaking is a blend of art and science, grapes can be a fun addition to your mini fruit garden in the right locations. Because of their vining nature, grapes require support in the form of a strong trellis, arbor, or pergola. Their cordons (the part where fruiting spurs and canes develop along vines) can be trained along wires on a fence or grown on overhead patio structures. The vines provide shade in the hot summer and defoliate in winter to let in more light. If you're growing grapes along a fence, install two sets of horizontal wires, 18 to 24 inches [45 to 60 cm]

Opposite: Grapes grow along fences and pergolas and keep a low profile in small space gardens.

apart, to train the cordons in the years to come. Plan your location carefully to ensure the vines will get enough sunlight and that you will be able to reach the vines for harvest and pruning.

Plant spacing: 6 to 8 feet [1.8 to 2.4 meters] apart

Plants per person: 3 vines (can be different varieties)

Sunlight: full sun

Ideal container specs: at least 18 inches [45 cm] deep, 16 inches [40 cm] in diameter, good drainage

Additional requirements: trellising for wall support or a T-post with wire cable guides for stand-alone growing

Fruiting period: late summer to early fall

CHOOSING VARIETIES

There are thousands of varieties to choose from, for different uses, climates, and soils. Traditional grape varieties are hardy between 0°F to -10°F [-17°C to -23°C] but newer and hybrid cultivars are hardy to -30 or -40°F [-34°C or -40°C]. Frost is a factor when choosing varieties, as some send out flower buds, or

Grapes set fruit in late spring and early summer for fall eating.

force budding, as a result of freezing of the first buds. (Varieties that aren't bred for frosty temperatures may break bud early and trigger forced budding of a second round of buds too soon once the first set has been damaged by frost.) Start by searching for varieties that grow well in your region, then decide how you plan to use the harvest. Fresh eating, juice, raisins, wine? Next, select the right option for the length of your growing season. Choose early-season varieties if you have a short growing season, and a range of early, midseason, and late varieties if you have a long summer and mild fall.

PLANTING GRAPES

Grapes prefer soil with a sandy loam that is well draining and slightly acidic. They require full sun—at least 6 to 8 hours per day. Amend soils with peat moss or aged manure to lower the soil pH if your soil is alkaline. Add compost or other organic matter to improve drainage, but do not add fertilizer to the planting hole. Avoid too much nitrogen, as that can promote leafy growth instead of fruiting.

Plant bare-root grapevines in late winter or early spring, and nursery-potted grapevines after the threat of frost is over. Dig a hole slightly deeper than the nursery pot and at least 12 inches [30 cm] wide. Amend the planting hole slightly as previously described. Soak bare-root grapevines in water for a couple hours before planting. Trim any roots that are too long for the planting hole or container. Place the rootball of potted vines slightly lower than soil level. For bare-root plantings, spread roots out and backfill gently. The graft union should rest above soil level. Most commercial grapes are sold as grafted varieties, but some nongrafted types are available. If you have chosen a nongrafted variety, plant the vine to match the soil level color change on the trunk. Water gently with kelp emulsion to remove air pockets and ease transplant shock. Grapes prefer to have warm roots so mulch isn't necessary.

Ripe grapes can be eaten fresh or frozen for a refreshing summer treat.

FEEDING AND HARVESTING GRAPES

Since the feeding schedule for grapes is going to vary depending on the varieties you have chosen to grow and the nutrients already present in your existing soil, consult the plant tag that came with your grapevine to learn more about that specific variety's care requirements. Generally speaking, grapes don't need fertilizer at planting time and may only need it after the first few weeks of growth, depending on your soil nutrient levels. Grapevines drive down deep roots for nutrients, and after a few years they may not need feeding at all. Young vines benefit from an application of compost yearly. Apply compost around the base of each vine, 1 foot [30 cm] away from the trunk. Test your soil for phosphorus and potassium levels to ensure they are sufficient for the plant's needs. Amend if needed; otherwise, let nature do her thing.

Watering requirements will differ as well, depending on soil structure, weather, and in-ground vs. container growing. Give new plants 1 inch [2.5 cm] of water weekly in dry climates for the first two to three years. Containers may need more frequent watering depending on drainage and temperatures. Cut back on watering in fall to prepare the plant for dormancy and pruning. Once established, grapevines may not need additional watering except during the dry season.

To harvest grapes, select bunches that are full-sized and rich in color. Taste a grape or two to know whether it is ready to pick or not. When it is sweet, it is ready to pick. Use pruning shears or scissors to cut the entire cluster from the vine. Remove any damaged or rotten grapes right away and refrigerate your harvest for up to two weeks. Store in an airtight container with a paper towel on the bottom

Use sharp shears to harvest bunches of grapes.

Prune grapevines yearly to encourage new growth and to train to a trellis.

to absorb moisture. Do not wash them until ready to eat unless they are very dirty. Pat washed grapes dry before storing.

PRUNING GRAPES

On newly potted grapevines, remove all vines except for the strongest two, one on either side of the trunk. Those will be trained as cordons over the next year. On bare-root plants, cut back all side canes but one, which will grow to be an extension of the main trunk. Provide light support for that cane to grow straight up. Next year it will form side shoots that can be trained along wires as cordons.

Summer pruning opens up the grapevine's leafy canopy to increase air circulation and sun exposure to help grapes ripen. Tackle summer grapevine pruning after clusters of fruit are set with pea-sized fruit. Growers at the Peaceful Valley Farm and Garden Supply recommend thinning growth to allow only "six to eight shoots per foot of canopy." They also suggest pruning back vines with fruit clusters so each vine has fifteen to twenty leaves. Cluster thinning helps reduce the burden on ripening fruit and prevents overbearing, which can tax a grapevine over time. Cut off clusters of fruit on vines that are up to three years old so that only twelve clusters remain. Prune away any deformed clusters as well. Consider trimming the bottom of each grape cluster to encourage larger fruit in that cluster.

Dormant season pruning takes place after the leaves have fallen or during the following early spring before budbreak. On year-old plants, encourage side branching for another set of cordons (if you plan to use a 2-wire training system) by cutting the top or terminal growth point above a bud once that vine reaches the height of your second, upper set of wires. Prune extraneous branches growing low on the trunk. Limit growth to existing and new cordons only. Do your research to learn specific instructions for pruning the particular variety you are growing. Each type of grape has different pruning needs. Much like cane berries, most grapes grow on the current season's fruiting spurs that developed on the previous season's canes, but that is not always the case. As you learn to identify spurs and distinguish between new and old wood, the job will become easier each year.

PASSION FRUIT

Passion fruit is a perennial vining crop that literally and figuratively covers a lot of ground quickly. Its vigorous vines are a great addition as a privacy crop along a chain link fence and can be used to cover a pergola for shade. Vines can grow up to 20 feet [6 meters] per year, so give them room and be prepared to prune often. Passion fruit is not frost tolerant, preferring not to dip below 32°F [0°C] so it's best for warmer regions. There are some cultivars bred to withstand temperatures in the upper 20s (-4 to 0°C), but in general this fruit wants a frost-free environment. The vines are evergreen although some of their leaves drop during cold winters.

You can find purple and yellow fruiting varieties for your garden. Yellow varieties are even less frost-tolerant than the purple one, but the fruit tend to be larger. Both can be grown in containers, but they are best grown in-ground due to their need for strong trellising. The skin is not eaten although it is often used for dying fabrics. The flesh inside isn't really flesh, but more like a membrane containing edible seeds and a tangy tropical pulp that tastes similar to guava. This liquid is great in smoothies and desserts or eaten fresh with a spoon.

Plant spacing: 12 to 15 feet [3.6 to 4.6 meters] apart, 8 to 12 feet [2.4 to 3.6 meters] apart in cooler climates

Plants per person: 1 plant can produce approximately 3 pounds [13 kg] of fruit per square foot after 1 to 3 years

Sunlight: full sun, with protected roots to keep them cool. In climates with extreme heat, they prefer partial shade.

Ideal container specs: at least 20 inches [50 cm] deep, 20 inches [50 cm] in diameter, good drainage

Additional requirements: strong trellising for wall support or thick wires attached to a fence with eye-hooks. Passion fruit is a vigorous grower, so trellises must be able to support heavy growth.

Fruiting period: Late summer to early fall

GROWING PASSION FRUIT

Passion fruit tolerates a range of soils between slightly acidic to slightly alkaline, but well-draining soil is a must.

PLANTING PASSION FRUIT

Passion fruit plants can be planted in late fall in warm-winter climates to overwinter while developing strong roots. Test your soil first to see if it has sufficient potassium levels before planting; then amend as needed. Prepare your planting area or container with rich potting soil, a little compost, and worm castings. Mix in an organic fertilizer with higher levels of potassium.

Opposite Top: Passion fruit takes up space but can be grown along a fence or pergola to be out of the way.

Opposite Bottom: Try passion fruit in smoothies or pour over ice cream.

Passion fruit becomes slightly shriveled when it's ready to pick and drops to the ground.

FEEDING AND HARVESTING PASSION FRUIT

As passion fruit grows in, guide the vines along the trellis. The vines will begin to flower and fruit one to three years after planting. The flowers are pollinated by bees, so be sure to plant beneficial insectaries nearby to attract pollinators to your garden. Once passion fruit gets going, it only needs to be fed two to four times per year. Beware of adding too much nitrogen fertilizer; otherwise, you'll have plenty of leaves without fruit.

To harvest passion fruit, wait until they turn from green to purple or yellow. Fruits will drop on the ground when ripe, or you can pick them when they change color. The pulp is sweeter when the fruits are slightly withered. Collect fallen fruits, wash and dry them, and store them on the counter for a few days. If not consumed by then, bag them and store around 50°F [10°C] for up to three weeks. You can freeze the pulp for later use as well.

PRUNING PASSION FRUIT

It's safe to assume that, unless you have unlimited space, vigorous growers such as passion fruit will need to be pruned on a regular basis. Trim back dead or damaged vines as needed using removal cuts (see chapter 8 under "Two Kinds of Cuts") and prune away any vines that have grown out of bounds or defy training to a trellis using reduction cuts (also in chapter 8).

In warm-winter climates, prune back all growth by one-third right after harvest. In cooler climates, prune back vines in early spring. Sanitize pruning shears before pruning to prevent the spread of disease.

The world of berries and smaller fruits will keep your garden interesting throughout the year. Now that we've covered these fruits that don't grow on trees, let's move on to the next steps, which include care and feeding of fruit trees. We'll also cover the basics of soil health and how nutrients perform in concert with soil microbes. This information will be helpful for taking care of both your fruit trees and small berries alike.

Feed your fruiting plants and trees to ensure an abundant harvest.

CHAPTER 7

Caring for Your Home Fruit Garden

Every fruit tree has needs, some more than others. With a foundation of healthy soil biology, in-ground fruit producers may only need to fertilize occasionally. In containers, however, fruiting plants require more frequent feeding. That's why it's important to learn to read signals from your plants to discern what they need. Let's start with the basics.

That bag or box of organic fertilizer on the shelf always lists three numbers on its package for NPK—nitrogen, phosphorus, and potassium, respectively. For example, the numbers on a box of organic fruit tree fertilizer might say 6-2-4. The "6" refers to the percentage of nitrogen in the formula. The "2" indicates the percentage of phosphorus, and the "4" tells you the percentage of potassium. But let's back up. What do each of these nutrients do?

Nitrogen is responsible for green leafy growth. Phosphorus helps plants flower and set fruit and develop strong roots. Potassium boosts a plant's overall vigor and disease resistance and helps with fruiting and flowering as well. Use this information as a starting point to diagnose nutrient deficiencies in your mini orchard. If leaves turn yellow and drop, a tree might need more nitrogen (we'll talk about overwatering, which can also be a factor, in a minute). If flowers form but drop off without setting fruit, it might be time to add phosphorus. If a tree looks stunted or weak, potassium might be needed. There are myriad other nutrients and micronutrients at play as well, but a home soil test kit indicating NPK results will narrow the focus to a starting point. Most store-bought organic fertilizer brands sell a formula for fruit trees, one for berries, one for veggies, and so on. Choose the right formulas for your fruits and see how the plants respond. If a plant struggles after that, look deeper into single nutrient amendments.

For example, yellow leaves with green veins can often indicate iron deficiency. Blossom end rot occurs when calcium is either inaccessible to trees or lacking overall. It's not just for tomatoes! It can happen to apples and citrus too. But before adding single nutrients to problem-solve, be aware that adding one nutrient can sometimes throw off the overall balance of garden soils. Many laboratories and university-based agriculture Extension programs offer inexpensive laboratory soil tests with specific recommendations for soil amendments based on the results. Embrace this opportunity! It's like driving with your eyes open. In addition to the soil test, try adding compost, worm castings, and compost tea first before reaching for the hard stuff. Compost and worm castings contain nutrients and micronutrients, as well as the microbes that process those nutrients and make them available to a tree.

Nitrogen promotes green growth on young trees and other plants.

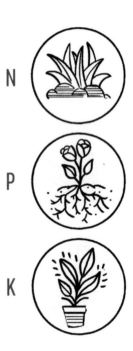

Use this graphic to remember the tasks that nitrogen, phosphorus, and potassium perform for plants.

Opposite Top: Sufficient phosphorus levels ensure flowering and fruiting.

Opposite Bottom Left: A citrus leaf with iron deficiency.

Opposite Bottom Right: Basic soil tests give you a starting point to know what amendments to add.

COMPOST AND COMPOST TEA

Fruit trees thrive in happy soil. Compost and compost tea make soil happy. Therefore, it's a good idea to use compost and compost tea as part of your fruit tree care regimen. Think of compost as an inoculum (reread chapter 2 for a refresher on the Soil Food Web and how to brew compost tea). It inoculates your soil with beneficial microbes and improves soil's ability to provide nutrients for fruit trees.

If you live in an urban or suburban area, your water supply is most likely treated by chlorine or chloramine, both of which kill microbes. So it's important to add compost around your fruit trees every so often to maintain high biological activity. It also helps to install a water filter on your hose or irrigation system to remove chlorine and chloramine if possible. There are hose-end filters available from garden supply catalogs that last through years of use.

Apply a ½- to 1-inch [1- to 2.5-cm] layer of compost around the base of each fruit tree, starting 4 inches [10 cm] away from the trunk and spreading out to the drip line. If you have mulch, gravel, or chip bark in place, pull it back before applying compost, then reposition your groundcover afterward. Depending on your soil needs you may only need to do this once or twice per year. Thin or heavily compacted soil will benefit from more frequent applications, up to monthly as needed.

Compost is even more necessary in the case of container planted trees. Nutrients wash away with water, and hot, dry days will cause microbes either to go dormant or die. In containers, soil levels decrease and compress over time. You can lift the rootball of a fruit tree out of the container, add 1 inch [2.5 cm] or so of compost or compost-rich potting soil to the bottom of the pot, and drop the rootball back in, filling in the gaps around the edge with more compost. *Boom!* You've inoculated the container with a fresh batch of microbes and given the tree something new to eat.

Compost tea serves as both a soil drench and a foliar spray that has two functions: It feeds the tree and helps keep pests at bay. Put freshly brewed compost tea (or put-to-sleep teas available over the counter) in a spray bottle or pump/backpack sprayer and mist the top and bottom surfaces of leaves. Leaves love to take in nutrients through their stomata, tiny pores or openings in the leaf surface. Compost tea coats leaves with beneficial microbes, which can attack pests and diseases to restore balance. You can also use compost tea as a soil drench, applied directly to the soil around the tree. Once it soaks in, microbes go to work rebuilding your Soil Food Web.

Compost is your friend. Use it abundantly.

Opposite: Adequate potassium levels result in vibrant, healthy trees loaded with fruit.

WORM CASTINGS

Worm castings are a fantastic tool to include in your fruit tree care arsenal. They are nutrient dense and a little bit goes a long way. But let's back up a minute. What exactly are castings, anyway? "Castings" is a civilized way of describing the excrement left behind by worms as they digest food scraps and soil organic matter. Yep, worm poop. But this excrement is going to feed your plants and fruit trees with NPK levels around 5-5-3. They are high in phosphorus to help roots develop and promote fruiting and flowering. They have decent levels of potassium for overall vigor. Plus, they have the obvious nitrogen hit for green leafy growth. But wait, there's more. Worm castings also contain iron, sulfur, and calcium. To top it off, these nutrients are water-soluble, making them more easily absorbed by a plant. If you want to avoid using store-bought fertilizer in your mini fruit garden, worm castings are a must.

Compost and worm castings fortify garden soil with more than just nutrients. They inoculate your soil with microbes too.

You can mix worm castings with compost before applying around the base of each fruit tree. You can also make tea with it to foliar spray and soil drench plants. As described, worm castings are rich, so you only need a few handfuls per bucket of compost.

The conversation about worm castings wouldn't be complete without mentioning the other benefit they provide: pest control. Turn to chapter 9 to learn how worm castings help ward off sucking insects in your garden.

OVER- AND UNDERWATERING

As mentioned in chapter 2, soil structure and texture are the main factors in determining how often and for how long you should water. Remember, fruit trees have deep root systems and prefer deep but infrequent watering. Most fruit trees prefer to be watered between once per week to once per month, depending on age. Container trees, if large enough, may do well with a once-per-week schedule, but may need additional water midweek in warm and hot weather. Start by adding 1 inch [2.5 cm] of water to the pot and test for depth of coverage after an hour. If the soil is dry a few inches [centimeters] down, add more water. Keep testing until you find water at the depth required for those tree roots. Make note of the number of inches [centimeters] you delivered and continue that practice. Older established trees benefit from a slow drip for a duration ranging from several hours to overnight.

Signs of overwatering manifest on fruit trees in a couple of ways. The most notable sign is yellowing leaves. When oxygen levels in soils drop due to flooding, a plant's ability to photosynthesize decreases. Plant roots can suffocate and die as well, but mainly it's the process of respiration that's interrupted when spaces between soil particles fill up with water and remain there too long. If you see an increase in yellowing leaves overall, check for leaks in your irrigation system and test for moisture to see how many days the soil remains saturated after watering.

Another sign of overwatering is wilting. Root rot sets in when trees have "wet feet." You may see fungi growing around the base of a tree. Mushrooms grow in consistently wet environments so let your soil dry more between waterings. Other indicators of overwatering can include fragile leaves that break or fall off easily.

Underwatering can cause death or partial die off as well. Signs of underwatering include brown, crisp leaves and unseasonal onset of fall color. Leaves can also turn yellow in drought situations, so that can be confusing. Always test your soil with a moisture meter or dig down and grab a handful of soil to see for yourself. The answer lies in the soil.

THINNING

If you recall back in chapter 5 under "One Last Thing," fruit removal at planting time is crucial for strong root development. Now let's talk about thinning the fruits, which is crucial for fruit production on established trees. Thinning is the act of reducing clusters of young fruit down to one or two fruits per spur. It eliminates competition and allows the remaining fruits to grow larger toward maturity. It also reduces the chance of fruit drop, which occurs when the tree aborts excess immature fruits it can't support. Keep in mind that some trees experience June Drop, self-thinning early in the season as a matter of course. Thinning is not as important on citrus trees as it is on stone fruits and pome fruits. Lack of thinning can result in tiny, flavorless fruits, or broken branches due to excessive weightbearing.

Thinning fruits is essential to making sure the harvest is large and healthy.

To thin properly, tackle the task when fruits are about 1 inch [2.5 cm] in diameter or smaller. Wait until after June Drop before thinning additionally. Remove any misshapen, diseased, or undersized fruits from each cluster. Some twist off easily while others require pruning with shears. It's emotionally challenging to remove perfectly good fruit from a tree, but this is a necessary task for continued tree happiness year after year. Aim for a distance of 4 to 6 inches [10 to 15 cm] between fruits after thinning. Go on, you can do this.

FEEDING AND HARVESTING FRUIT TREES

Much like watering, the fertility needs of a fruit tree will depend up on the soil texture and how quickly nutrients drain away. In-ground and container-grown fruit trees have different needs as well. The following includes general guides for tending your fruit trees, which you can adapt depending on your growing situation and the trees' responses.

CITRUS

As mentioned briefly in chapter 5, citrus trees prefer a lower to neutral soil pH, between 6.0 to 7.0. Slightly acidic soil provides the ideal environment for proper nutrient uptake in citrus trees. When planted in alkaline soils, citrus can have difficulty accessing certain nutrients. Try the trick in the "Citrus Treatment" sidebar to help drop the pH slightly if you have alkaline soil. You can also use amendments such as sulfur to lower soil pH but use them sparingly to avoid over-application, which can trigger other soil issues down the line.

Iron deficiency manifests as yellowing leaves with green veins. Magnesium deficiency looks similar, but the green part of the leaf looks more like a Christmas tree. Low sulfur levels present as a pale yellow/green color spread evenly across new growth. Other nutrient deficiencies result in deformed fruit or thicker skin. If your leaves have watersoaked spots and the fruit is hard or dry, you could have a boron deficiency. It can be challenging to diagnose a single nutrient deficiency. For help, bring cuttings of the leaves and fruit to your local nursery for advice or consult a university agriculture site for images of common citrus problems.

Citrus Treatment

If your citrus tree is looking sad, try this trick to boost growth, vitality, and fruit production.

Step 1. Remove mulch or gravel from around the tree to expose bare soil.

Step 2. Apply a ¼-inch [.6-cm] layer of worm castings around the tree, starting 4 inches [10 cm] away from the trunk out to the drip line if possible.

Step 3. Mix organic fruit tree or citrus fertilizer into the worm castings with your fingers. Use the quantities as listed on package directions.

Step 4. Cover the top of the worm casting/fertilizer mixture with a layer of acidic planting mix.

Step 5. Water well and then restore mulch or gravel as need.

The Citrus Treatment can be applied monthly until you see improvement. If the suggested treatment doesn't improve leaf color after several applications, you may need to look to single nutrient amendments for further help.

Citrus fruits will release easily from the tree when ripe.

To harvest citrus fruits, wait until they are full and evenly colored. The fruit should give slightly when you squeeze it and should separate easily from the stem when it is ripe. Twist or tug gently to see if it's ready. Citrus stores well on the tree so you don't have to harvest right away. To encourage a new round of flowering and fruits, however, it is a good idea to remove any fruit remaining on the tree toward the end of the season. You can juice lemons, limes, and oranges and freeze the juice in small containers or ice cube trays for later use. Citrus is also shelf stable for several weeks and can be refrigerated.

POME FRUITS

Apples, pears, and quinces each have their own set of care instructions but do have some similarities. All three prefer to be planted late fall to early spring if bareroot, and in fall if potted. They are all late summer/fall-ripening fruits and many varieties can be picked firm for storage. Early in the season, sometime from early summer to midsummer, take time to thin apple and pear fruit clusters (quinces do not require thinning) as illustrated in the "Thinning" section. This is also a good time to protect against coddling moth and apply barriers to each fruit, if using. See chapter 9 for details about proper protection against this pesky intruder.

APPLES

Crisp apples are a staple of fall and winter. There are hundreds of varieties available for a wide range of climates. Apple trees prefer loamy to sandy loam soils but will tolerate clay soils with good drainage. They require regular watering starting from early spring through the growing season. Apple trees like a little bit of shelter and grow well on the north side of buildings as long as they still get six hours of sunlight per day.

Some apple tree varieties are self-fruitful but most need a pollinizer for adequate production. Apple trees need sufficient nutrients for fruit production including the big three (NPK), magnesium, and calcium. Early and soft-flesh-type apples are considered light feeders, whereas crisp-flesh and cooking apples tend toward higher nutrient requirements. Feed apple trees in early spring through midsummer in climates with short growing seasons. Warm-winter climates and gardens with poor soil benefit from additional feeding through summer. Apply a layer of mulch to help retain moisture in the soil.

To harvest apples, wait until the color is full before testing for ripeness. Cup the apple in your hand and twist up. If it releases from the stem easily, it is ripe. If it does not, leave it a few more days and try again. Taste one apple before picking the rest. Your taste buds will be the best judge. If it's too tart, wait awhile before testing again. You can pick storage apples at the firm stage for storing and allow them to ripen on the counter when you're ready to eat them. Use apples in baking, applesauce, pies, jams, and fresh eating.

PEARS

European and Asian pears are other late summer/ fall fruits to include in your garden. Asian pears produce earlier in the summer and grow in warm-winter climates where European pears will not thrive. While pears are among the fruits that tolerate soggy or clay soil and some shade, they prefer well-draining soil with a slightly acidic pH around 6.5 in a full-sun location. Most pears require a pollinizer to fruit, but there are self-fruitful varieties available. Both have a similar upright growth habit similar to apples and can be trained into a number of shapes.

Opposite: Pick fruits before critters can steal them, but make sure they are ripe first.

Lift rather than twist to harvest pome fruits.

Keep young pear trees watered well; they do not like to dry out. Feed your pear trees in early spring before they start to leaf out. Use a balanced organic fruit tree fertilizer mixed with compost and pay attention to nitrogen levels. Pears are a Goldilocks fruit; they do not want too much nitrogen, nor too little. If leaves start to yellow, increase the nitrogen amount, but if you see new growth in excess of 2 feet [60 cm] per season, cut back on the nitrogen.

To harvest, take note that European and Asian pears behave differently. Asian pears are left on the tree until they are completely ripe, and the color has darkened to maturity. Regular pears must be picked prior to full maturity, when they are green and very firm, lest they develop mealy flesh. Pick the fruits by lifting upward without twisting or pulling, which can damage the fruiting spur. The best way to know if pears are ready is to taste them, and if the fruit doesn't remove easily from the tree, it isn't ready. European pears will be firm but sweet when they are ready. Store pears in temperatures between 32° to 40°F [0°C to 4.4°C] for weeks at a time. Bring European pears to room temperature to finish ripening as needed.

QUINCE

Quinces differ from apples and pears in that they have a bushy, weeping growth habit instead of an upright one. They are self-fruitful and require a long, hot growing season to ripen fully and become sweet. In cooler climates quinces are most often cooked because they don't reach that full maturity before frost hits in autumn. They are best baked into jams, jellies, and pastries with sugar to sweeten them.

Quinces are similar to apples and pears in that they prefer slightly acidic soil with a pH around 6.5. As with apples and pears, feed quince trees in early spring before budbreak and apply a thick layer of mulch around the base of the tree, starting 4 inches [10 cm] away from the trunk, extended out to the drip line. Water as you would apples and pears, making sure to check for proper drainage, as quinces don't like wet feet.

Quinces are best if left on the tree as long as possible. They store nicely on the tree, especially since they are persnickety when it comes to storing them. Harvest fruits in the fall when the color has shifted to yellow. They will still be firm in short-season gardens. Avoid covering the fruits in storage, and space them apart so they don't touch, since they bruise easily. They will last a couple of months if stored in a cool, dark place, but can begin to wither in a few weeks when refrigerated.

STONE FRUITS

Ah, stone fruits. Summer isn't the same without these succulent, sweet flavors at the table. Stone fruits are called this because they have a pit in their centers. They produce summer through early fall in most cases. Apricots and cherries have a shorter harvest period than peaches, plums, and nectarines, but they are no less enjoyable when they are in season. You will be able to find self-fruitful varieties for your mini fruit garden with a little bit of research. Since many are not self-fruitful, make sure you have enough room for two if you favor varieties that require a pollinizer. It is particularly important to choose varieties with the appropriate chill hours for your climate, as stone fruits will not produce at all outside of their comfort zone.

As with most fruit trees, stone fruits prefer to be planted as bare-root plants in late fall through winter, and as potted trees in fall. They develop strong roots over winter and leaf out in spring. It may take between three to five years for young stone fruit trees to begin to bear fruit. This category of fruit tree is often the target of squirrels and other curious, hungry critters so plan to protect your stone fruit trees if you want to see a harvest.

APRICOTS

In many ways, apricots are the princesses of the stone fruit family. They tend to flower early, which puts them at risk in frosty climates. In hot temperatures they can suffer pit burn (when the flesh around the pit turns brown and softens). And if they get wet after pruning, they can die. Still, some say they are easier to grow than peaches and nectarines. Apricots prefer climates that are dry in spring and they like a sunny but sheltered location. They grow in nutrient-rich, well-draining soil, and tolerate neutral to slightly alkaline soils with a pH between 6.5 to 7.5. Most apricots are self-fruitful and grow well in containers.

Feed apricot trees with a balanced organic fruit tree fertilizer in late winter/early spring but protect blossoms from frost damage with insulated garden fabric if there is a threat of frost where you live. Maintain a mulch layer around the base of the tree starting 4 inches [10 cm] away from the trunk out to the drip line. Water the trees deeply but infrequently in spring through the growing season. After June Drop, thin excess fruits to allow 3 to 4 inches [7.5 to 10 cm] between fruits.

Apricots are ready to harvest when they are fully ripe and the flesh begins to soften. Give each fruit a gentle twist to test for doneness. They are ripe if they come off the stem easily. Apricots are fragile and don't last long after picking, so plan to process or eat them within a couple days of harvest. You can preserve them by canning, freezing, or drying.

CHERRIES

There are two types of cherries to choose from, depending on your desires and plans for use. Sweet cherries are grown for fresh eating, and acid or sour cherries are grown for cooking into pies, jams, and other confections. There is a third category, the Duke cherry, which is a hybrid between sweet and sour cherries, that have been in cultivation since the late-1700s. The Duke cherry can be used for fresh eating as well as cooking. Most sweet cherries are not self-fertile, so they require a pollinizer in order to produce fruit. Sour cherries, on the other hand are mostly self-fertile. There are newer sweet cherry hybrids on the market that are self-pollinating, but in most cases, you will need two trees or a multi-fruit tree for successful fruiting.

Grow your cherry trees in well-draining soil that retains water but isn't soggy. They can be grown in containers as long as you choose dwarf varieties since cherries are vigorous growers. They require ample nutrients and compost to produce abundantly, and regularly testing for potassium levels will help keep you aware of any need to add more. Feed with a balanced organic fruit tree fertilizer in early spring before budbreak and mulch sufficiently around the base of the tree. Loose (sandy) soils and container-planted trees will require repeat applications of fertilizer during the growing season. Good news! Cherries don't need thinning, so you can let them go wild.

Cherries fall into the category of fruits that should be picked fully ripe. They do not ripen off the tree, but they may soften as they begin their descent toward decay. Immediately pick any cherries that have split and enjoy them right away. Harvest cherries with shears or scissors to avoid damaging the fruit or fruiting spurs and because cherries store better with stems attached. If you feel confident that you won't damage either fruit or spurs, you can hold the stems and twist up to remove the fruit from the tree. Place your unwashed harvest (or washed and thoroughly dried) in a sealed container with a dry paper towel on the bottom. Place them in the refrigerator shortly after harvest to keep them fresh longer. Cherries can be frozen, dried, canned, or processed with sugar for pie filling and other baked goods.

NECTARINES AND PEACHES

Nectarines have one recessive gene to thank for their differentiation from peaches. That gene gives them smooth, thin skin instead of peach's fuzzy velvet. Otherwise they are the same (okay, nectarines have a slightly lower calorie count than peaches, but who's counting?). Both are available with white or yellow flesh, and there are freestone (the pit removes easily) and clingstone (Easy pit removal? Not so much.) varieties of both. Cooking experts say that freestone varieties are better for freezing, whereas clingstone types are more suitable for canning. Most varieties are self-fruitful and don't require a pollinizer.

It bears repeating that it is important to choose varieties for your climate's chill hours, otherwise you'll be watering and feeding a tree with nothing to show for it. Plant nectarines and peaches in soil with a pH from 6.5 to 7.0 in well-draining soil. They benefit from amending the soil with well-rotted manure or compost a month or so prior to planting the tree.

Feed your nectarine and peach trees in late winter/early spring and through the summer with an organic fruit tree fertilizer containing ample levels of potassium. They benefit from liquid potassium supplements in midsummer as fruits develop. Surround the tree with a thick layer of mulch, carefully placed 4 inches [10 cm] away from the trunk, out to the drip line. You may need to protect your crops with either floating row cover (for frost protection) or netting (for squirrels, birds, and other hungry critters). Thin young fruits to one fruit per cluster.

Opposite: Wait to pick cherries until they are fully ripe.

To harvest nectarines and peaches, give them a squeeze to know if they are ready to pick. They will give slightly to pressure at the stem end. Cup the fruit in your hand and gently twist. If they are ready, they will come right off. These fruits can be picked slightly early in the firm stage and will soften on the counter if you run the risk of wildlife stealing them before you can harvest them fully ripe. Keep in mind, though, that they do not increase their sweetness after picking. Store peaches and nectarines on the counter just until they're soft, then transfer them to the refrigerator for longer storage. Or you can store them immediately in the fridge and set them out on the counter to soften two or three days before you want to eat them. Allow clingstone varieties to sit out for a couple days before canning them as that will make the skin easier to remove.

PLUMS AND GAGES

In discussing plums and gages (aka, greengages—green-skinned plums), let's also include hybrid pluots and damsons. Damsons, a cousin of plums, are not as widely familiar in the Americas as they are in Great Britain and Europe. Regardless, they all belong to the same family and have a similar growth habit. There are three categories in which these fruits fall: European, Japanese, and American hybrids. American hybrids tend to be the hardiest for colder regions, with European as a close second, followed by Japanese as the most tender.

Plums and gages, like other stone fruits, prefer slightly acidic, well-draining soil and full sun exposure. Some are self-fertile and don't need a pollinizer. Non-self-fertile varieties bloom at different times, so it is important to choose the right pairing or select trees from a grouping of varieties that all bloom at the same time to ensure pollination.

Feed your trees in early spring when they begin to set fruit, and test for nutrients throughout the growing season to amend as needed. Thin fruits early in the season, after June Drop, when they reach about 1 inch [2.5 cm] in diameter. Protect your crop with netting, either over the entire tree or around clusters of fruit. Like other stone fruits, critters love to sample plums, gages, and their hybrids as fruits ripen.

To harvest plums, gages, and hybrid varieties, wait until the color is fully developed and the fruit comes off easily with a slight lift upward. The fruit will give slightly when you squeeze it but can be picked firm for softening on the counter. Some trees will ripen their fruit all at once or within a two-week period, so be prepared to eat and process a bumper crop during that time. Store the harvest in a refrigerator or in a cool, dark and dry location free of drafts. You can purée the fruit with strawberries and a little sugar for fruit leather, jams, pie filling, or compote. Can or freeze sliced pieces or halves of fruit or dehydrate them for snacking on the trail.

Opposite Top: Ripe stone fruits come off easily with a twist when they are ready.

Autumn begins the countdown toward pruning season for many fruit trees.

CHAPTER 8

Pruning for Production, Size, and Structure

Let's admit it: Pruning is scary. It takes courage to pick up a pair of loppers and cut away living branches. There's so much that could go wrong, right? Maybe not. As the old saying goes, knowledge is power. And in this case, knowledge also brings courage. If you tackle pruning in stages, it is much less daunting than you think. You're a sculptor observing the lump of clay before you. The tree before you is the clay. Study it. See how the branches cross, trace the overall shape with your eyes, notice the flow of air in the negative spaces between branches. This tree is yours to mold. Here are a few starting points to guide you along.

TREE SHAPE

Trees in a commercial fruit orchard are often pruned to a shape called open vase or open center. This keeps trees shorter and branches grow outward, making it easier to harvest from a ladder. Home gardeners, if they have room, can choose this shape, but often there isn't room to allow branches to spread wide in a small space. The best choice for home mini fruit growers may be modified central leader or pyramid, which fits well in narrow spaces; espaliered or fan, which hugs a wall or fence; or bush shaped, which can be kept compact without creating shade or a space-hogging canopy. These are more compact choices for confined spaces.

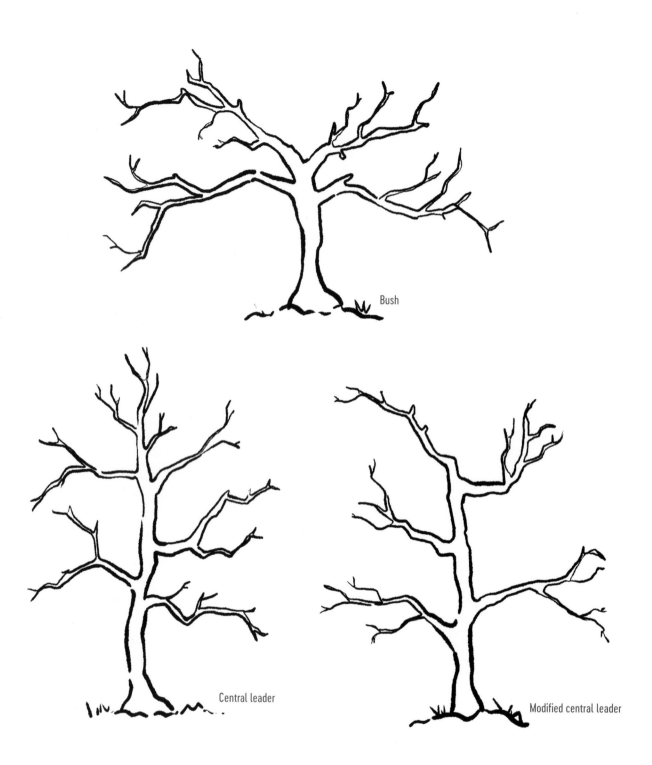

Bush

Central leader

Modified central leader

Choose the best shape for your space. There are no "shoulds" here; just what fits best for you.

Once you decide which shape is best for you, learn how to control that shape with proper pruning techniques specific to the species. Young trees need training in their first three years. The decisions you make early will determine the size and shape of the tree for years to come. Don't be afraid to mold a young tree to your desired shape. Most of the heavy and detailed pruning occurs in winter when trees are dormant, although summer pruning plays a role after the tree finishes fruiting. Use the following techniques as a guide.

THE THREE DS

The three Ds are "Dead, Diseased, and Disorderly." If all you do is check these three boxes, you're in good shape.

DEAD

A dead branch is usually obvious. It's brown or sometimes white, as on citrus trees. The leaves are brown or fallen. It may snap easily when it's bent. If you aren't sure whether a branch is dead or not, cut the tip off and examine the cross section. If there is any trace of green on the inside or around the edges, it's still alive. If it's brown all the way through, it's dead. Cut back farther until you start to see green in the cross section. You can also scratch the young bark with your fingernail to expose the green cambium layer beneath. If you don't see any green color, cut all the way back to the main branch or truck with a removal cut. What's a removal cut? We'll get to that in a minute.

DISEASED (OR INFESTED)

Disease shows up in many ways: sap oozing from a branch, a swelling in the trunk, deformed leaves, discoloration. It's important to remove affected branches to prevent spread to the rest of the tree. It is also important to sanitize your pruning shears or loppers between each cut. Disease travels on pruning shears, so dip the blades in alcohol after each cut and wipe it dry before moving to a new location.

Dead citrus tree branches often turn white, making them easy to identify.

Cross sections solve the mystery as to whether a branch or twig is dead or alive.

Sanitize, Sanitize, Sanitize!

Another way to sanitize your pruning equipment is to fill a spray bottle with straight alcohol and keep it on hand during pruning sessions. Spray both sides of your blades between cuts, and when you're pruning a new tree.

Sanitize pruning shears between cuts to keep disease from spreading.

DISORDERLY

While dead and diseased are straightforward, disorderly is more subjective. Disorderly can look like a branch extending too far into a pathway. It can be top growth that has gotten too tall to reach without a ladder. Disorderly is most often seen as crossing branches that rub together when the wind blows, suckers (which are fast-growing shoots from the rootstock that don't produce fruit), and drooping branches weighed down by an abundance of fruit. It can also be an overgrowth of young branches that prevent healthy air circulation.

In this category, the pruner must choose which branches to keep and which to eliminate. This is where observation is key. Look at both crossing branches and follow them up or out to see where other crosses occur along that branch. It will become clear that one is more of an obstacle than the other. Use a removal cut to eliminate the one causing more trouble. Cut away any suckers from the rootstock, doing your best to cut below the soil surface. Prune back long drooping branches with reduction cuts.

Watersprouts are one example of "disorderly."

Crossing branches can lead to damage on tree bark, making the tree vulnerable to disease.

Pruning Espaliered Trees

Espaliered trees require diligent pruning in their first three years. Train branches to sturdy support wires and don't be afraid to use removal cuts to eliminate stragglers. Use 10- to 12-gauge wire spaced 18 to 24 inches [45 to 60 cm] apart horizontally to train trees to espalier. Pears, apples, and Asian pears are great choices for espalier because they produce fruiting spurs on short shoots. After planting the tree, cut the trunk off just below the first wire, then train the resulting growth as follows: Choose, as the trunk, the most upright branch to continue straight up to the next set of wires. Then choose the two best laterals to attach horizontally to the wires. Repeat the process for the upper set of wires until you have as many levels as you wish.

Year 1

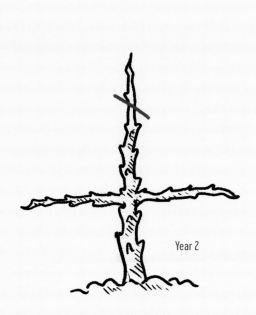

Year 2

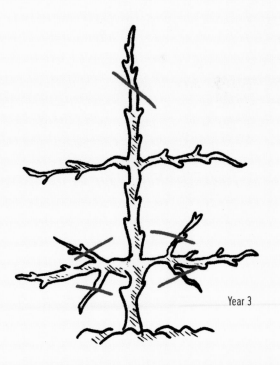

Year 3

The first three years training espaliered trees are the most important.

TWO KINDS OF CUTS

REDUCTION CUTS

A reduction cut reduces the length or height of a branch by cutting it back to an outward-facing bud or to a younger or lateral branch. Cut on an angle parallel with the bud, about a ½ -inch [1 cm] above a bud or branch.

Here's some nifty science to explain how apical dominance works in branches. The tip of a branch exudes a hormone called "auxin" that prevents other buds below it from becoming leader branches. Auxin flows with gravity, so an upright growth tip will subdue everything below it. Reduction cuts eliminate the apical growth tip of a branch, which removes the auxin at the same time. This removal triggers new growth of buds farther down the branch, allowing them to fill in gaps or bald spots in the crown (canopy) of a tree. Use this type of cut to shorten the height of a tree over time rather than all at once. It may take a three-year plan to reduce the height and canopy of older trees that have been allowed to grow unfettered. In younger trees, reduction cuts help train the tree for future growth.

Opposite: Removing all downward growing twigs from citrus opens up space for air circulation.

REMOVAL CUTS

A removal cut eliminates an entire branch by cutting back to the branch collar, close to the trunk. For example, if two crossing branches are rubbing together, use a removal cut to eliminate one of them completely. If you want a defined tree trunk and a topiary-shaped crown, use removal cuts to eliminate low-growing branches to define the trunk.

For large branches, see Figure 1 for guidance on how to remove the branch without damaging the tree. First, cut a short notch into the underside of the branch with a pruning saw to prevent damage to the bark. Then, cut the branch off 1 foot [30 cm] or so away from the trunk to remove the weight of the branch before making the final removal cut (A–B). Last, cut the remaining branch off just outside the

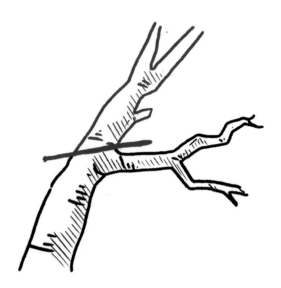

A reduction cut reduces the length or height of a branch.

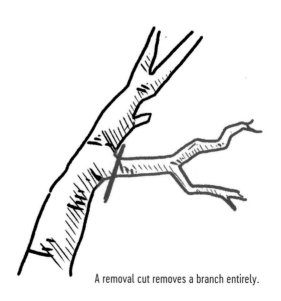

A removal cut removes a branch entirely.

branch collar, which is indicated by a swelling and gathering of the bark at the base of the branch (C-D). Do not cut into the branch collar. The branch collar will grow over the wound to seal it, but if damaged it cannot perform its function. The wound will remain exposed to disease and further damage over time.

Use *reduction* cuts to keep a tree the *size* you want it to be. Use *removal* cuts to keep it the *shape* you want it to be and to keep the canopy open and healthy. Each fruit tree has its own set of pruning requirements, so do your research for details beyond these basics.

For example, some trees fruit only on new wood, whereas others fruit on old wood. Some fruit on spurs. It can get confusing. Pruning gets more specific once you learn where your tree grows new fruit. New wood is a different color than old wood; the bark of new wood is often tinged with red or light green. If you prune away all the new wood on a tree that only produces on new wood—no fruit. See why it's important to do your research for your specific tree? The information is out there and relatively easy to find. When you're ready, dive in and take good notes. You will find supplemental guidance in the coming pages to cover the basics.

For what it's worth, it's highly recommended to take a pruning class every year if only to bolster your courage to tackle annual pruning. Right after a pruning class, you'll feel ready for anything and clear-headed enough to make a first pass. Check off Dead, Diseased, and Disorderly. Use reduction and removal cuts to shape and reduce. Then double check your research for pruning specific trees and go for it. Before you know it, you'll be done, and your trees will look pretty darn good.

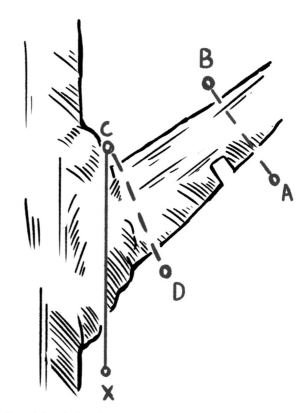

Figure 1. Note the branch collar and avoid it when making the final cut to remove a branch.

An improper cut has been made too close to the branch collar and ridge bark. This will prevent the wound from healing properly.

SUMMER PRUNING

To maintain your fruit trees at "home orchard height" between 6 to 10 feet tall [1.8 to 3 meters], summer pruning can be a key strategy for fruit trees that grow too vigorously. As mentioned, the bulk of specific fruit tree pruning occurs in fall or winter. But summer pruning allows you to reduce height once the fruiting season is over. Dry summertime is also the safest time to prune apricot, apricot hybrids (apriums, plumcots, and so forth), and cherries to avoid spreading diseases. Now is the time to remove skyward-reaching branches that would require a ladder to reach the harvest if their growth is left unchecked.

Summer pruning is controversial, in that it can suddenly expose areas of the tree that were shaded to the summer sun, increasing the risk of sunburn or sunscald. Also, some experts say to prune only 10 percent while others encourage 20 to 30 percent reductions, depending on the type of tree. You'll find guidance here, but always do your tree-specific research before diving in. Let's go through the process step by step.

First, schedule time in mid- to late summer when the fruit tree has finished producing for the year. Next, identify the branches to remove or reduce. If it helps to tie twine or yarn around those branches to keep them straight, go for it. But don't worry about it too much. Summer pruning doesn't have to be perfect.

Make a first pass around the tree to reduce branches that have grown into pathways, other trees, or garden beds. Use clean, sanitized loppers to cut back branches to an outward-facing bud (see "The Three Ds") around the circumference of the tree. Reduce the branch length by at least one-third and as much as half, as needed.

Now it will be easier to access those sky-ward-shooting branches and watersprouts (which are fast-growing but unproductive vertical shoots that grow from older branches) at the top of the tree. To reach the top branches, you may need a ladder. No swivel chairs please; use the right tool for the job. Anchor your ladder on solid ground and enlist the help of a friend or neighbor to hold it in place if you're pruning on a slope. Use reduction cuts to prune the selected branches back to an outward-facing bud, cutting away at least one-third of the branch length. This will help stimulate new growth for next year.

Last, take a moment to remove any sucker shoots or broken branches at this time. Check the trunk for new, whiplike sprouts of growth (called "suckers") and remove them with pruning shears as desired. These anomalies should be easier to see once the overgrowth is cut away.

Remember, sometimes you'll need to make more than one pass to complete the job. That being said, if all you do is reduce a tree's height and circumference in summer, you can tackle more detailed pruning (removing crossing branches, dead wood, and so forth) in winter.

PRUNING SPECIFICS

Now let's get down to the nitty gritty about how and when to prune fruit trees. In the following pages you'll find advice for each group of fruit tree: citrus, pome fruits, stone fruits, and other fruits including mulberries, figs, avocados, and more. It's still worth mentioning that you will benefit from researching your chosen variety for any pruning nuances or deviations from the norm. If you are looking for pruning tips for small fruits such as berries, grapes, and passion fruit, turn to chapter 6.

To prune your fruit trees, you'll need a clean, sharp pair of loppers, shears, and, in some cases, a pruning saw. What you won't need is any type of paint, tar, or sealant. Paint is often used on tree trunks to prevent sunscald but don't paint over open wounds after pruning. It isn't necessary. Trees will heal themselves if pruned properly and that healing is hindered if you apply a coating over the wound. If you prune at the appropriate time of year, when dry weather is in the forecast, the tree won't need any help sealing over the wound.

PRUNING CITRUS

When it comes to pruning citrus, you can count on the Three Ds to get you most of the way there. Citrus is fairly forgiving if you stick to removing branches that are dead, diseased, and disorderly. The best time to prune citrus is after the tree finishes fruiting but before it begins to flower again. There is a short window if your trees happen to produce fruit twice per year but pay attention and seize the opportunity when you see it. If you see flowers forming while there is still fruit on the tree, you can harvest all the remaining fruit (juice and freeze for later) and prune quickly. The tree will recover and send out new flowers shortly thereafter. Here is a check list to review as you inspect your citrus trees for pruning needs:

Keep citrus tree interiors open by removing dead and downward-growing branches.

Pruning Multi-Fruit Trees

The main concern with multi-fruit trees is that, inevitably, one variety will try to take over. Usually the branch that receives the most sun will begin to outgrow the others. It's up to you to keep things in check. As Tom Spellman of Dave Wilson Nursery says, "You can always control the overgrowth." In other words, it's much easier to prune back the overachiever than it is to wait for the underdogs to try and catch up.

1. Scan the overall shape and take note of any broken or dead branches, especially interior growth that has died back. Use pruning shears to cut away any dead branches (they may be whitish) to open up the space. You may need to get under the tree like a mechanic under a car to view the interior branching.

2. Look for growth tips with curled or damaged leaves, scale, aphids, and so on. If you can cut off the affected growth tip without sacrificing next year's fruit, do it. Make note of pest and disease issues and consult chapter 9 for remedies.

3. Identify watersprouts—those branches that shoot straight up and never produce fruit. Use removal cuts to prune them back to the source. Check the trunk and root zone for suckers growing out of place and cut those away, below soil level if possible.

4. Continue to prune for size and shape; use reduction cuts to shorten long branches back to lateral branches that are closer to the trunk. Use removal cuts to prune out crowded growth pointing up or down from lateral or scaffold (main) branches.

Those are the basics for pruning citrus trees. Now let's move on to pome fruits.

Pruning Hedgerows and Closely Planted Trees

Hedgerows and trees planted in the same planting hole (combination plantings) require more training at a young age to prevent crossing branches, poor air circulation, and crowding. Get to work as branches begin to touch. Prune away the central growth of combination plantings, and keep hedgerows evenly sized so one tree doesn't overtake the others. Be diligent about removing water sprouts, and dead or diseased branches to prevent the spread.

PRUNING POMES

Apples, pears, Asian pears, and quinces are perhaps members of the most diverse group when it comes to pruning. Some varieties fruit on spurs while others fruit on branch tips. Some fruit on old wood from 6 to 10 years old, while others fruit only on new shoots. Timing differs depending on the tree's shape. This is why research on pruning your specific variety is key. But let's keep it as simple as possible.

APPLES

Most apples are spur-bearing; they bear fruit on two-year-old wood on short spurs that live between 8 to 10 years. But some varieties are tip-bearing instead, producing mostly on new wood near the branch tips. There are also partial tip-bearing varieties that produce mainly on the branch tips of last year's growth, but also on some spurs. Determine whether your variety is spur-, tip- or partial tip-bearing before you prune the tree. Spur-bearing trees are more compact (meaning, they are better suited for mini fruit gardens) and require less pruning than tip-bearing types. All are best pruned in winter.

Always start with the Three Ds, using Steps 1 through 3 in "Pruning Citrus," and then move on to these specifics for apples:

1. Use reduction cuts to shorten new growth on main branches by about 25 percent on spur-bearing varieties. To prune tip-bearing apple trees, look for side shoots off lateral branches, and use reduction cuts to shorten the lateral branch to a lower side shoot. That will trigger new growth for fruiting in coming years.

2. Prune sub-laterals and new side shoots back to four to six buds (make sure the bud you cut back to is outward facing).

3. Spur-bearing types can become crowded over time so prune away very old spurs to make room for new growth.

Cool Tip: Apples have an upright growth habit. If your apple tree is only producing leaves near the branch tips, you can bend long branches downward and anchor the tip with string to the ground. This process is called "subtending." It will keep the auxin in the branch tip (remember auxin flows with gravity) and the rest of the branch will be free to send out new shoots and fruiting spurs.

PEARS

Asian and European pears both produce on two-year-old wood, mostly on the tips of short branches or spurs that live between 6 to 8 years for Asian pears, and between 8 to 10 years for European pears. They produce occasionally on longer branches laterally or terminally (on the tip of each branch), but most pear varieties are spur-bearing.

Prune pears as you would apples, in winter, ideally focusing on pruning to create shorter branches with fruiting spurs. Asian pears require heavier pruning than European pears. In both cases, use the Three Ds to get basic pruning out of the way and then follow these specifics:

1. Use reduction cuts to shorten the length of lateral branches, leaving about 10 inches [25.5 cm] of last year's new growth to remain. Make your cuts above an outward-facing bud.

2. Use reduction cuts to prune side shoots and sub-lateral branches back to two or three buds. This will help create more fruiting spurs for future fruit.

3. Use removal cuts to prune out overcrowded spurs or those no longer producing. You can also thin individual clusters of fruiting spurs down to just two or three per spur.

QUINCE

Quince produces fruit mostly along the length of a long branch, and to some degree at the tips of branches. Fruits form on new wood and therefore only require light pruning in winter to thin out old wood year to year. Start with the Three Ds and then refer to the instruction under "Apples" for pruning tip-bearing type trees.

Plums fruit on spurs. Learn to identify them to spare them when pruning.

PRUNING STONE FRUITS

Stone fruits produce on either longer branches or on short spurs. The number of productive years of those spurs differs among species, ranging from 1 to 12 years before they should be pruned off. Timing is also important. Cherries, apricots, and plums are best pruned in late summer after the growing season with minimal to no winter pruning since they are susceptible to diseases if pruned in wet weather. Nectarines and peaches are hardier and can be pruned in late winter. To determine where to prune, let's look at the fruiting habits of each type.

APRICOTS

Apricots produce fruiting buds laterally (along the length of branches) on short spurs and to a lesser degree on longer one-year-old shoots. Their spurs only produce fruit for three years, so yearly pruning is required to foster new growth and future fruiting spurs. You can also prune away two-year-old branches that bend downward. This bears repeating: Avoid pruning apricots in winter. In summer, start with the Three Ds and then make another pass to do the following:

1. For young trees, use reduction cuts to shorten main branches by about half in summer. Locate an outward-facing bud and cut back to ½ inch [1 cm] above it.

2. Use reduction cuts to shorten sub-lateral and side shoots to about 6 inches [15 cm] long. This will help trigger new fruiting spurs.

3. Use removal cuts to eliminate nonproductive older fruiting spurs.

CHERRIES

Cherries, for the most part, produce fruiting buds laterally on short branches and spurs that are two years old. They also produce some fruiting buds on long branches of last year's growth. Their spurs bear fruit for 10 to 12 years. Therefore, cherries require only light pruning of old fruiting spurs to maintain production. Overall, however, cherry trees have a vigorous apical dominance, so reducing long branches by 30 percent in late summer will trigger new lateral growth of future fruiting spurs. Sour cherries and sweet cherries set fruit differently, so read up on your variety for specific pruning instruction. Follow the Three Ds under "Pruning Citrus," and then proceed with the steps found under "Apricots."

NECTARINES AND PEACHES

Nectarines and peaches produce laterally on long branches. They only fruit on the prior year's shoots. Because of this fruiting habit, you will need to annually prune away branches that bore fruit to encourage new growth for future crops. Unlike their tender cousins, prune peaches and nectarines in late winter or early spring as they begin to show new growth. Start with the Three Ds under "Pruning Citrus," and then follow the steps under "Apricots."

PLUMS AND GAGES

Plums and gages produce laterally on short shoots and spurs, and less so on long branches. Their fruiting spurs are productive for between 5 to 8 years. European plums are more vigorous growers than Japanese varieties, so regular pruning is more important with European types. As plum trees reach 3 years old, they need less pruning than their younger counterparts. Use steps 1 through 3 of "The Three Ds" under "Pruning Citrus," then find step-by-step instructions under "Apricots."

Don't be afraid to tag fruiting branches with twine or paint as needed to denote removal at the end of the season. Research your specific variety to verify proper pruning techniques and timing in case it falls outside normal guidelines.

OTHER PRUNING

AVOCADO

Avocados can grow to be an enormous size but choosing a dwarf variety will save you time pruning down the line. Avocados have a tip-bearing fruiting habit, which can be tricky because their branches can grow long and droopy. If you must prune the branch tips or do more than just a minor adjustment here and there (which can be done at any time of the year), do so in early spring or in summer no later than July. Otherwise the tree won't have time to recover to produce new fruiting shoots in time for fall. Another reason to avoid pruning in hot weather is that your tree may incur sun damage on newly exposed areas. Be diligent about using clean pruning equipment as avocados are susceptible to disease. Every avocado grows in its own way, so take these guidelines as a loose starting point and then make decisions based on the way your tree is behaving.

1. Scan the tree for the Three Ds and use removal cuts to eliminate dead and diseased wood. Disorderly wood includes low-growing branches that block access to harvesting fruit, and watersprouts shooting straight up.

2. Prune symmetrically, meaning if you reduce or remove a branch off one side of the tree, do the same on the other side. Balance is key to a happy, sturdy tree that can withstand wind and other influences. Spread out major pruning over several years to maintain tree health.

Opposite: When it comes to plums and gages, it's all about the fruiting spurs.

3. To increase sunlight for lower branches, consider pruning "little windows" into the upper canopy. Choose upper branches on the sunny sides to remove. This should be done with careful consideration to avoid overexposing the trunk to sunburn.

4. Inspect the tree for overexposure and paint the bark of those areas with diluted white latex paint to avoid sunburn.

FIG

Fig trees can be pruned to suit any size of garden, be it a central leader, bush, open center, or espalier. Whichever shape you choose, be sure to keep the tree at a height that is easy to harvest. Figs can get out of hand if growth is left unchecked, and it may take several years before the tree produces fruit. Figs are also invasive and tend to sprout up all over the place (from scattered seeds left behind by rodents or other hungry bandits).

Many varieties produce a "breba" crop, the first of the season in summer, on the previous year's wood, and then a second crop in fall on new growth. The breba crop sets fruit the previous fall and overwinters after the tree drops its leaves. Naturally, heavy pruning over winter will drastically curb the first (breba) crop the following year, but pruning will not affect the second crop. If you prune your fig trees more heavily while they are young, you may not need to prune them much once they mature. To encourage two harvests in one year, follow these pruning specifics:

1. Inspect the tree for the Three Ds before tackling other issues. Scan for and remove suckers around the base of the tree; also remove volunteer fig sprouts that have popped up out of bounds. Pull them before they become too large to remove without equipment.

2. Prune only about one-third of the branch tips per season using reduction cuts, leaving two-thirds of the canopy to produce fruit. Reduce those branches back to three nodes or buds to encourage new, shorter growth next year.

3. Use removal cuts to thin overcrowded shoots, and any lateral branches that are growing at a less than 45-degree angle from its main branch.

4. If you perform a heavy pruning, paint the trunk with diluted latex paint to protect against sunburn.

GUAVA

Guavas are generally grown in a bush shape because they can topple easily in inclement weather if they're allowed to grow too tall. When the trees are young, use reduction cuts to tip-prune the branches in late winter or early spring to encourage a bushy growth habit. Then follow the Three Ds under "Pruning Citrus" for basic pruning guidelines. You can prune each branch by 50 percent in the years that follow.

Opposite: Figs are a great choice for small gardens, though they'll have to be overwintered carefully in colder climates.

MULBERRIES

Mulberries may sound like they belong in chapter 6 with other berries, but they grow on a tree so their pruning guidelines belong here with their fruit tree counterparts. Mulberries can take years to get established but they are worth growing because they do not transport well to market. Homegrown is the best option if you love to eat these delicate sweet-tart fruits. Fair warning: mulberry trees can grow to 30 feet [9 meters] tall, so dwarf varieties are a must for a mini fruit garden. There are weeping varieties that stay relatively compact as well. Prune mulberries in winter when they are dormant, unless grown as an espalier. Those should be pruned in summer. Prune mulberries as you would apple trees. (See "Apples" under "Pruning Pomes.")

PERSIMMONS

Persimmons, if unimpeded, can grow to upwards of 20 feet [6 meters] tall and wide, so pruning and training is key at a young age. They bear fruit on new growth, producing laterally along longer branches. However, here's the thing to understand about where persimmons fruit: They generally form flowers and fruit on the tip end, on the last three or four buds of the branch. So treat persimmons as tip-bearing fruits when it comes to pruning (see "Apples"). Prune lightly in winter to avoid cutting off too much of the one-year-old growth.

Persimmons can suffer dieback if branches don't get enough sunlight. Use removal cuts to open up the canopy to allow more sunlight through. Heavy pruning of scaffold branches will trigger new growth and future fruit. Employ summer pruning to keep trees small (see "Summer Pruning"), being cognizant to avoid pruning away too many new shoots.

POMEGRANATES

Pomegranate trees can be trained several ways. In cold climates, their chances of survival increase if they're grown either as a multi-trunk tree (three to six trunks at most) or shrub form. In warmer climates, however, trim off all suckers from the base of the tree, and train to one main trunk. Pomegranates produce fruit laterally along short second-year wood. They will develop a cascading shape over time and may need thinning with summer pruning to keep the canopy open. Wear gloves to protect yourself from the thorns found on pomegranate branches. Use the Three Ds to keep the tree in shape, and prune in winter or early spring, before budbreak. Reduce the length of lateral branches by one-third and leave three to five shoots on each branch.

Now it's time to move on to pest control, and disease prevention and treatment in chapter 9. Together with proper pruning, integrated pest management helps you get the most out of your mini fruit garden without reaching for chemical sprays and other harsh treatments.

Use the techniques in this chapter to ensure your fruit trees and plants stay pest free throughout the season.

CHAPTER 9

Managing Pests and Diseases

Now that your mini fruit garden is growing, you may run into problems between planting and harvest time. Over the years, fruit trees can develop diseases or fall victim to a number of setbacks. Using integrated pest management (IPM), this chapter aims to find a balance between predator and prey, and to increase your chances of harvesting high-yields of delicious, pest-free fruit.

What's integrated pest management? It's the concept of using our knowledge of nature's ecosystems (habitats) and lifecycles to find environmentally friendly, sustainable, or, better yet, regenerative solutions to pest and disease problems. This might be a good time to revisit the "Soil Food Web" section in chapter 2 as it plays a serious role in IPM.

The following pages will help you diagnose problems and pests that can take all the fun out of gardening. With a little knowledge, the right protection, and time, you and your fruit garden will survive and thrive. Additionally, to fend off many of the pests listed here, employ the help of beneficial nematodes.

PEST CONTROL

Nothing smarts more than a stolen harvest. When squirrels take a single bite out of your fruit and then toss it carelessly on the ground, you're bound to run the gamut of emotions. Anger, frustration, sadness, even helplessness. We share this planet with our fellow inhabitants, and they need to eat too. But we work hard for a bumper crop, and it's not wrong to want it all for ourselves. Let's start by identifying several common pests in a fruit garden. We'll also explore ways to keep each of them at bay.

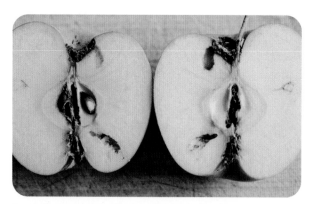
One apple maggot makes for more than one bad apple.

APPLE MAGGOT FLY AND CODLING MOTH

These fruit tree pests are similar in a few ways: Both most commonly deposit eggs on apple trees, but can infest pears, quince, plums, cherries, and, on rare occasions, blueberries and apricots as well. Both overwinter in soils. But they do have their differences. Apple maggot fly (*Rhagoletis pomonella*) is a black-and-white striped fly smaller than a ¼ -inch [.6-cm] long, and codling moth (*Cydia pomonella*) is a ½-inch [1-cm] brown, velvety moth. The larvae of both burrow into fruit, but only codling moth caterpillars leave behind insect frass (fruit detritus pushed out of the hole). Apple maggots leave behind a clean hole. Codling moths do damage first, starting in late spring and rearing their ugly heads again in late summer. They can produce four generations in one year. Apple maggot flies deposit eggs in early summer through fall and produce only one generation per year. Codling moths not only pupate in the soil, they often find a home in cracks in tree bark, making them harder to eradicate.

The key to managing both pests is a three-pronged approach: interruption of the life cycle, debris clean up, and physical barriers.

INTERRUPTION OF THE LIFE CYCLE

Since these critters pupate in the soil over winter, you can apply predatory nematodes (*Steinernema carpocapsae* and *S. feltiae* for coddling moth) or parasitic wasps (*Trichogramma* spp. for apple maggot fly) during the season to kill them before they emerge as adults or parasitize them at a young age, respectively. Apply an organic horticultural oil over winter to suffocate pests incubating in tree bark.

DEBRIS CLEAN UP

Fallen fruit can harbor codling moth caterpillars and apple maggot larvae. Be diligent about disposing of dropped and damaged fruit throughout the season. Different rules apply depending on where you live, but many cities, counties, and states have laws requiring on-site destruction (controlled burning) rather than disposal to prevent spread. Damaged fruit can be hot composted at temperatures above 130°F [54.4°C] to kill the insects.

Codling moths can be stopped by covering the fruit early in the season.

Lady beetles love to feast on aphids and other sucking insects, including the Asian citrus psyllid.

Asian citrus psyllid leaves telltale curly waxy tubules behind.

The Asian citrus psyllid is a vector for citrus greening disease.

PHYSICAL BARRIERS

Install sticky traps in early spring to attract the pests away from your precious fruit and install pheromone lures to confuse the pests as they try to mate. Use maggot barriers, which look a lot like nylon footies, to cover individual fruits or clusters of fruit when they are about 1 inch [2.5 cm] in diameter. Mesh, paper, and plastic fruit protection bags also offer some benefit. Kaolin clay is another physical barrier that coats the surface of fruits to form a protective layer, preventing entrance to maggots and caterpillars.

ASIAN CITRUS PSYLLID

The Asian citrus psyllid (ACP), *Diaphorina citri*, is a vector for Huanglongbing, also known as citrus greening disease. This flea-sized bug is a sap-sucking insect similar to aphids and others mentioned in "Sucking Insects." The difference is that ACPs carry bacteria that transmit a disease to citrus trees, causing infected trees to die. For years there has been no cure for Huanglongbing. If a citrus tree is infected, it will die. Hope once resided in an experimental IPM treatment, that of a parasitic wasp called *Tamarixia radiata* that feeds on nymphs once they hatch. But this parasitic wasp is not in wide use, nor is it available to home gardeners at the time of this writing. A five-year trial at UC Riverside, California, shows promising results with an antimicrobial peptide derived from Australian finger limes, which are naturally resistant to citrus greening disease. The study showed this peptide to be more effective than pesticides and antibiotics and is a natural plant derivative that is safe for humans. Time will tell how well it works.

While this cure is still in the early stages of release, an otherwise grim diagnosis does not bode well for the citrus industry and home citrus growers. Arborists and many Master Gardener programs now recommend against growing citrus at all; instead, they suggest growing tropical fruits such as guavas, papayas, and loquats. However, according to University of California Division of Agriculture and Natural Resources, the Asian citrus psyllid "is attacked by many natural enemies, including lady beetles, lacewing larvae, syrphid larvae, minute pirate bugs, parasitic wasps, spiders, and birds. These natural enemies

Bring on the Beneficials

To attract the beneficial insects mentioned above to your mini fruit garden, grow a patch of flowers that includes members of the *Umbelliferae* family, such as alyssum, dill, cilantro, queen Anne's lace, and yarrow.

do not eradicate the psyllid, but they help reduce psyllid populations." Given this information, think twice before using Neem-based horticultural oils and pyrethrin sprays, as they can negatively affect beneficial insects.

What home orchardists can do in the meantime is control the ant population. As with other sucking insects, ants will protect and farm the psyllid. Therefore, if gardeners reduce the ant population, that will in turn help reduce the spread of the ACP. Use boric acid-based bait stations to reduce the ant population around your citrus trees. Place ant stations at the base of each tree and check regularly to replace them as they dry out.

BIRDS

Birds know when crops are ripe before gardeners do. Half of a berry crop may be pilfered away before anyone realizes it's time to harvest. The best deterrents for birds include physical barriers and distractions that throw them off guard.

PHYSICAL BARRIERS

Bird netting is a nearly invisible way to protect berry bushes, strawberries, grapes, and highly desirable fruits such as stone fruits, pomegranates, and figs. Use stakes to elevate bird netting above the shrub, vine, or small tree, and secure the netting to the soil with U-pins. Vining crops and fruit trees with small leaves tend to grow through the netting, but stakes set a short distance away will allow protection without interference.

SHINY OBJECTS AND DECOYS

Birds become disoriented when light shines close to their target. Hang strips of mylar reflective tape or old CDs and DVDs in your garden to bounce sunlight back at birds. Eventually the reflective surfaces will fade but it lasts for a couple months at most, which is enough time to harvest your crops. Predator decoys such as scarecrows, fake snakes, and owls lose potency after a while, but if you shift them around your garden or change the position every once in a while, they will continue to deter birds.

DEER

In a mini fruit garden, you are less likely to encounter deer due to the limits of your physical space. However, deer can mow a garden down to stumps in no time, and they can damage tree bark in a visit or two. If you live where wildlife includes these beautiful four-legged creatures, protection is essential not optional. Physical barriers and odor repellents are your best bets. You can also strategically plant deer-resistant crops to keep them at bay.

Old CDs can deter birds from stealing your fruit.

Damage from deer on a fruit tree.

PHYSICAL BARRIERS

Deer fencing is a thicker version of bird netting that can stand up to 8 or 9 feet [2.4 or 2.7 meters] tall, since deer can jump nearly 8 feet [2.4 meters]. Alternatively, you can build a much shorter double fence, one 4-foot-tall [1.2-meter-tall] fence that is 4 to 5 feet [1.2 to 1.5 meters] in front of another 4-foot-tall [1.2-meter-tall] fence. Deer have trouble navigating tight spaces so the double fence will deter them. For fruit trees, consider tree guards to protect the trunks of young trees. They are available as mesh panels, spiral wraps, or plastic tubes that keep tree bark safe from harm. You can remove these barriers as the tree grows.

ODOR-BASED REPELLENTS

Deer do not like strong fragrances such as garlic, strong-smelling soap shavings, chilis, putrefied eggs, or dairy. There are sprays on the market that provide protection with odors that are toned down for humans but that are still effective for deer.

DEER-RESISTANT PLANTS

If you have room, plant deer-resistant flowers around your mini fruit garden. Bulbs such as daffodils and irises are unappealing to deer, and plants with strong fragrances such as alliums and hyacinth repel them. Lavenders, sages (salvias), marigolds, rosemary, and mints turn them off as well.

Gophers can destroy tree roots. Protect trees at planting time or be prepared to set traps.

GOPHERS AND MOLES

When it comes to burrowing animals, you might need to prepare yourself for extreme measures. Moles are insectivores that usually hunt for grubs, worms, and insects. They primarily disrupt lawns and may cause upheaval to garden plants, but they leave tree roots alone. Gophers, on the other hand, gnaw away at tree and shrub roots from underground, destroying any hopes of future harvests. Gophers are omnivores, eating anywhere along the food chain from worms and soft-bodied insects to food crops and plant material. If you live in an area where foxes, skunks, owls, hawks, and snakes also live, you're in luck. These are natural predators of gophers and moles. Otherwise, the best options for protection against these burrowing creatures are physical barriers and traps.

PHYSICAL BARRIERS

Gopher baskets are metal mesh containers that gardeners can install in the hole before planting a tree. These baskets protect the rootball with wire that is too thick for gophers to gnaw through. Roots can grow through the cage material, but the core rootball will remain protected. Gopher baskets are available in 1-, 5-, or 15-gallon [3.8-, 19-, or 57-liter] sizes. Half-inch [1-cm] hardware cloth is another option for homemade barriers. You can install a barrier around the perimeter of the garden down to a depth of 30 inches [50 cm] to keep moles and gophers from entering the area. Extend the mesh above the ground by 6 inches [15 cm] to ensure zero entry.

TRAPS

Unfortunately, prey animals such as gophers and moles reproduce quickly. Therefore, the motto of "live and let live" will result in an overabundance of burrowing creatures in your garden. Trapping is unpleasant but you may feel up to the task after you discover one too many ravaged fruit trees or berry bushes. You can choose between live traps or kill traps.

Gophers prefer to run in tunnels along retaining walls. Entrances are usually set apart from mounds, where you'll find a sinkhole instead. Set the trap in the entrance and cover the opening with something to keep it dark inside. Tie the trap to a stake firmly secured nearby. This will make it easier to retrieve the trap and the kill later. Moles have deep tunnels that surface near volcano-shaped mounds. Set mole traps on the soil surface of an active tunnel near a mound.

ONE MORE THING

If moles are not damaging your crops but are simply disrupting the soil, you can apply beneficial nematodes (*Heterorhabditis bacteriophora* or *Steinernema riobrave*) or spray a castor oil treatment to rid the soil of grubs. Then the moles will have nothing to feast on and will move elsewhere.

GRASSHOPPERS

The grasshopper is another insect that incubates in garden soils over winter, after which they emerge in late spring and summer the following year. There are several approaches to reducing populations and protecting your crops from them.

ALTER THE HABITAT

Grasshoppers love grassy patches, so if you have the space, you can grow a cover crop of wheat or rye off to one side as habitat to draw them away from your garden. Hang suet cakes in the area to attract kestrels and other birds that eat grasshoppers. Since grasshoppers lay eggs in the soil to incubate over winter, you can loosen and slightly turn topsoil in winter to expose eggs to the elements, where they will desiccate and die. Use bird netting to cover small fruit trees or shrubs that are under attack until populations subside.

BIOLOGICAL CONTROLS

Grasshoppers are susceptible to a protozoan called *Nosema locustae* and to a fungus called *Entomophthora grylli* that infect the young and turn them belly up. Organic applications for *Nosema locustae* are available to treat an area to eradicate grasshoppers in the early stages. Older grasshoppers are more resistant to the *Eg.* fungus, so try to apply it when you first spot them in the garden. Some gardeners trap grasshoppers and drown them in soapy water. Others cut them in half with pruning shears when they discover them. The less brave (this author included) use a jet blast of water to remove them from treasured plants or squish them underfoot.

LEAFMINERS

Leafminers are the larvae of several different insects that burrow into a leaf's surface and tunnel through, leaving behind a squiggly trail visible on the top or underside of the leaf. They are primarily a cosmetic nuisance, but if left unchecked they can hinder a fruit tree's growth or open the tree to disease.

BIOLOGICAL CONTROLS

Foliar applications of beneficial nematodes *Steinernema feltiae* and *Steinernema carpocapsae* both attack insect larvae and render them useless. Early in the season you can also release a parasitic wasp, *Diglyphus isaea,* to control populations before they overwhelm your garden. If problems still persist,

Leafminers cause cosmetic damage on fruit tree leaves.

Peach tree borer is tiny but causes a world of trouble.

A plum curculio in action.

apply an organic horticultural oil that contains Spinosad, which is a bacterium the larvae ingest to their detriment.

PEACH TREE BORER

Damage from a peach tree borer is characterized by a type of "sawdust" deposit at the entrance to a borer hole. This damage appears most often near the base of the trunk, but it can be found on the rootstock that appears above ground as well. The moth (*Synanthedon exitiosa*), a beautiful metallic blue-winged insect, deposits eggs on the tree bark in the summer. Its larvae burrow into the tree and tunnel around until the next spring, when they then emerge to pupate in the soil or on the bark of the trunk. While they are inside the tree, they cause damage that can kill a younger tree.

PHYSICAL BARRIERS

Paint the trunk of an affected tree to reduce potential cracking and make the tree's bark less ideal for incubation and egg laying. Horticultural and Neem oil sprays have been shown to be effective in interrupting the life cycle if applied to the lower part of the trunk and soil between midspring and fall.

BIOLOGICAL CONTROLS

Timing is everything when it comes to biological controls. Once borers burrow into a tree, they are almost impossible to treat. However, in spring and fall you can inject beneficial nematodes into the entrance and apply as a foliar spray to the trunk and soil when you see cracks and "sawdust" frass. Consider releasing the *Trichogramma pretiosum* moth egg parasite to parasitize the adults when they are present. Pheromone disrupters are effective to interrupt the mating cycle as well.

PLUM CURCULIO

Plum curculio (*Conotrachelus nenuphar*) is found in specific regions east of the Rocky Mountains in North America. This beetle attacks stone fruit trees, pome fruit trees, and some blueberries by laying eggs inside the fruit, feeding on the fruit's flesh, and causing brown rot. They prosper in temperatures over 70°F [21.1°C] arriving at bloom time and can produce up to two generations in one season, surviving up to seven weeks. Females cut crescent-shaped scars into the skin of growing fruit and deposit eggs inside, leaving behind a brown spot that can develop as a depression or a bump in the fruit.

PHYSICAL BARRIERS

Use maggot barriers in early spring during fruit set when fruits are 1/4 inch [.6 cm] diameter or apply kaolin clay to protect fruits from infestation (see "Physical Barriers" under "Apple Maggot Fly and Codling Moth" for details). If the kaolin clay washes off during rains, it must be reapplied to be effective. The good news is that plum curculio activity dies down during wet weather. Monitor your trees and shrubs diligently between bloom time and when petals fall, as this is when activity is highest.

BIOLOGICAL CONTROLS

Beneficial nematodes (*Steinernema riobrave*) help treat beetles and weevils of all sorts, including the plum curculio. Apply to the soil and tree surfaces. They can kill the insect within 48 hours of application and can parasitize the pest to continue populating with more nematodes long after the host is dead. It is safe for direct application to fruit trees.

SOW BUGS, PILL BUGS, AND BEETLES

Roly-poly is another name for a pill bug (*Armadillidiidae*). A sow bug (*Oniscidea*) looks like a pill bug but it doesn't curl up in a ball when you touch it. Small beetles such as strawberry sap beetles and picnic bee-

Beetles can be good and bad. Level the playing field in the battle of beetle vs. fruit.

tles range in color from brown to black, some with spots, some solid colored. They eat your small fruits before you can harvest them and are especially fond of strawberries. All of these insects are attracted to overripe and decaying matter. They then find your ripening young fruits and feast on them as well.

DETERRENTS

Remove any overripe fruits from the garden to prevent attracting these insects in the first place. Consider removing mulch from around these fruits as well, as mulch *is* decaying matter. You can place baited traps, such as decaying fruit, vinegar, water/yeast mixtures, or stale beer, away from your garden to lure them away. Change the bait every few days until the infestation abates.

DIATOMACEOUS EARTH

Diatomaceous earth (DE) is fossilized, single-celled organisms from a billion years ago. To gardeners it feels and looks like flour. But to sowbugs, pillbugs, and other tiny insects, it feels like shards of glass. It pokes holes in them, causing them to desiccate and die. DE becomes inert when wet, so be sure to sprinkle it around your plants on a dry day between waterings. You will need to reapply after watering if the insects persist.

JAPANESE, GREEN JUNE, AND FIGEATER BEETLES

Depending on where you live, these iridescent green beetles are different. Japanese beetles (*Popillia japonica*) are found east of the Mississippi in the U.S., as are June or green June beetles (*Cotinis nitida*). Fig or figeater beetles (*Cotinis mutabilis*) are found in the southwestern United States and Mexico. The grubs of all three look similar: large, white, crescent-shaped, ribbed larvae with translucent or dark heads. Those grubs are root feeders and they will show up in your lawn or compost bin, as well as in garden soils. Homesteaders call these larvae "chicken shrimp" because they make great snacks for backyard chickens (Note: Japanese beetle grubs are poisonous to chickens but figeater and green June beetles are not.). The adults eat the fruits, flowers, and leaves of many garden crops. The best way to manage them is to interrupt their life cycle.

TREATMENTS

Bacterial applications such as milky disease—sometimes called milky spore (*Paenibacillus popilliae*)—or Bt (*Bacillus thuringiensis*) work to some degree if you choose the right bacterium for the particular beetle you have. Milky disease mainly works on Japanese beetles but is less effective on figeater beetles. The grubs must consume the bacteria in order for it to work, so several applications during the season may be needed. The best time to apply is in the fall when the grubs are feeding on roots before hibernation. Beneficial nematodes (*Steinernema riobrave*) and kaolin clay also treat and protect against beetles, respectively.

SQUIRRELS, RACCOONS, RATS, MICE, AND VOLES

Four-legged critters can be anything from a minor nuisance to a persistent plague. Squirrels love to nibble on fruit and nut trees, and steal strawberries one by one. Raccoons are carnivores and are most likely

Animals that seek out your garden produce usually visit at night, but some critters can steal in broad daylight.

digging in your garden for grubs when they uproot your newly planted seedlings. But they also love nuts and grains, so you'll need a strategy to keep them out. Rats and mice squeeze through tiny spaces and climb to new heights to sample your figs, berries, stone fruits, and more. It's enough to drive a gardener mad.

Since some states and provinces have laws against trapping pests out-of-season, or killing squirrels and racoons, we'll stick with humane options here.

LIVE TRAPS

Live traps are cages with lures to attract racoons and squirrels into them. The door closes and voila! You can relocate the disappointed prisoner to a wild space on the other side of town. According to Havahart, which makes live traps, "Sweet foods and fatty meats are some of the best baits" to capture racoons. For squirrels, try nuts, corn, or cereal as bait. And for rats, cheese and peanut butter are tried-and-true baits. Set your trap where the interlopers frequent and check it daily for a catch. If the trap goes several days without a catch, shift to a new location. Make sure to avoid placing live traps on slopes or near water. Prisoners can move the cage during a struggle and may end up drowning.

No Poisons, Ever!

First off, let's agree that poison is never the right choice when it comes to pest control. The food chain is vast, and many of these creatures become food for larger animals up the chain. If your cat is a good mouser, keep her active and alive by avoiding poisons in the garden at all costs. Many cats eat rats in their entirety, leaving nothing but the tail as evidence. So no poisons—ever. Got it?

Place rat traps perpendicular to buildings and retaining walls where rats travel frequently.

Drape small trees with bird netting and secure to the ground.

KILL TRAPS

There are no laws protecting rats, mice, or voles, and they repopulate so quickly that kill traps are the best option. Rodents are smart and learn how to avoid kill traps, or to trigger them without being caught in order to grab the bait. So it's important to stay diligent and move your traps around regularly. Keep the element of surprise alive. Rats and mice run along borders such as retaining walls and buildings. Voles do the same in shallow, serpentine, underground tunnels, but also run aboveground in tall grasses. It's worth noting that voles rarely depart from their well-trodden runways, so choose locations with evidence of activity for your trap.

For rats and mice, set your traps perpendicular to the wall with the bait closest to the wall. As mentioned, cheese and peanut butter are ideal baits for rat and mouse traps. There are electronic types available, but they can be expensive and don't function properly if they get wet. Use 15 to 30 traps at one time until the population decreases and damage stops. If pets are outside during the day, deactivate the traps and reset them at night when pets are once again safely inside. Place a reminder by the door, such as a broom handle or plush toy, to deactivate the traps before letting Fluffy outside in the morning. Do this four or five nights in a row and the population will dwindle for a stretch.

For voles, use baits such as sunflower seeds or small-sized nuts, bread and butter, or oatmeal mixed with a nut butter. Place bait both in the trap and around the area to attract them. Check the trap daily and reset as often as needed to catch more. Plan to use between 12 to 25 traps to reduce the population over several weeks.

PHYSICAL BARRIERS

In addition to setting traps, physical protection is your best tool to prevent theft and damage to fruits. Drape bird netting either over the entire fruit tree or around clusters of ripening fruit to prevent access to nibbling marauders. If you drape bird netting over the entire tree, you must secure it at the bottom, either against the trunk or to the ground, to prevent entrance from below. Also see "Physical Barriers" under "Apple Maggot Fly and Codling Moth" for details about using nylon footies and other protective bags. Sometimes deterrents containing peppers, garlic, or rotten eggs will keep voles at bay.

Sucking insects such as mealybugs damage trees and hamper growth.

Leaf-hoppers are sucking insects that continue to weaken an already weak plant.

SUCKING INSECTS: SCALE, APHIDS, MEALYBUGS, WHITEFLIES, AND LEAF-HOPPERS

Scale can be brown, pink, or white, and they form a shell to seal themselves to a stem or leaf. Aphids arrive in many colors such as white, gray, red, green, and black. Mealybugs are white or gray and have a characteristic furry coat reminiscent of a small sow bug covered in snow. Whiteflies are tiny winged white flies that leave behind a trademark of white cotton-candylike webs on the undersides of leaves. Leaf-hoppers are often green but they can have stripes or colorful thoraxes on occasion. They jump from leaf to leaf and create stippled damage on leaf surfaces.

These five pests look very different, but they all equally suck. Literally, they use their mouthparts to pierce the tender stems and leaves of fruit trees and suck out plant fluids. They all have a symbiotic relationship with ants, which provide "taxi services" in exchange for the sweet honeydew the insects excrete. There are several approaches to treating sucking insects. Let's explore.

FORTIFY YOUR SOIL

When pests show up it's a sign that your tree or plant is weak. Therefore, the first line of defense is to boost plant vitality by fortifying the soil with beneficial microbes. Compost, compost tea, and mulch will feed soil microbes and inoculate under-populated soils with the microbial task force a tree needs to thrive. Compost is not only a mild fertilizer, it is an inoculum, adding billions of additional soil microbes to help the tree process nutrients more readily. Compost tea (applied both as a foliar spray and a soil drench) coats leaf surfaces with microbes to fight invaders on a microscopic level. Mulch feeds soil fungi, allowing fungi to make long-chain hyphal connections to nutrients and minerals buried deep down. All these amendments boost plant vitality and allow a tree to outcompete pests.

Homemade worm castings are the best source of free fertilizer and provide pest control help too.

WORM CASTINGS

Worm castings are not just a great fertilizer; they act as a pest control as well. Worm castings contain "chitinase," an enzyme that breaks down chitin (the substance that forms the exoskeletons of many soft-bodied insects). Plants take up the chitinase from the worm castings and when sucking insects ingest it, the chitinase begins to work, and the pests degrade. Add a ¼-inch [.6-cm] layer of worm castings around the base of any suffering tree and you'll see improvement in a couple weeks. Repeat the process monthly as needed.

HORTICULTURAL OILS

Organic horticultural oils act to coat and suffocate sucking insects. They have a mineral oil base that smothers aphids, mealybugs, whiteflies, and scale.

Some oil sprays are sold in combination formulas with dormant oils, fungicides, or treatments for non-sucking insects such as coddling moth.

While many horticultural oil product labels state they are safe to apply at any time, some must be applied during a fruit tree's dormancy.

DISEASES

Diseases weaken plants and trees, and often strike when trees have been neglected or undernourished. Rubbing branches can expose the cambium layer below the bark and grant access to diseases. Pruning with contaminated shears or pruning at the wrong time of year can leave trees vulnerable as well. Other disease may appear due to environmental disturbances or imbalances in soil biology. Here are the most common to protect against.

FRUIT	SUSCEPTIBLE TO:	NOTES
Apple	Anthracnose*, armillaria rot*, blossom wilt*, brown rot*, powdery mildew*, apple scab*.	*See "Fungal Diseases"
Avocado	Anthracnose*, armillaria rot*, Phytophthora**, root rot**, sunblotch viroid**, verticillium wilt*	*See "Fungal Diseases" **See "Virus/Other Pathogen Diseases"
Blueberry	Blueberry virus**, botrytis*, mummy berry*, Phytophthora**, powdery mildew*, rust*, stem blight*, Septoria leaf spot*	*See "Fungal Diseases" **See "Virus/Other Pathogen Diseases"
Cane berries (blackberry, raspberry, and so on)	Armillaria rot*, botrytis*, cane blight*, cane spot*, fungal leaf spot*, powdery mildew*, virus**, rust*	*See "Fungal Diseases" **See "Virus/Other Pathogen Diseases"
Cherry	Bacterial canker***, blossom wilt*, brown rot*, fungal leaf spot*, shot hole disease*, silver leaf*	***See "Bacterial Diseases" *See "Fungal Diseases"
Citrus	Anthracnose*, armillaria rot*, botrytis*, citrus canker***, Huanglongbing /citrus greening disease^, powdery mildew*, sooty mold*	*See "Fungal Diseases" ***See "Bacterial Diseases" ^See Chapter 9 "Pest Control / Asian Citrus Psyllid".
Currants and Gooseberry	Botrytis*, fungal leaf spot*, Phytophthora (dieback)**, reversion disease**, rust*, mildew (downy)*	*See "Fungal Diseases" **See "Virus/Other Pathogen Diseases"
Fig	Botrytis limb blight*, various rot diseases including brown rot*, mosaic virus**, smut*	*See "Fungal Diseases" **See "Virus/Other Pathogen Diseases"
Grape	Armillaria root rot*, botrytis bunch rot*, cane and leaf spot*, corky bark**, crown gall***, leaf roll**, Pierce's disease ***, powdery mildew*, red blotch**, sour rot*	*See "Fungal Diseases" ***See "Bacterial Diseases" **See "Virus/Other Pathogen Diseases"
Guava	Anthracnose*, guava wilt*, rust*	*See "Fungal Diseases"

Mulberry	Armillaria root rot*, bacterial blight***	*See "Fungal Diseases" ***See "Bacterial Diseases"
Olive	Armillaria root rot*, leaf spot*, olive knot**, Phytophthora**, verticillium wilt*	*See "Fungal Diseases" **See "Virus/Other Pathogen Diseases"
Passion fruit	Anthracnose*, bacterial spot***, fusarium wilt*, leaf mottle**, mosaic virus**, scab*, Septoria leaf spot*, various rot diseases (including Phytophthora)**, woodiness**	*See "Fungal Diseases" ***See "Bacterial Diseases" **See "Virus/Other Pathogen Diseases"
Peach/Nectarine/Plum/Apricot	Bacterial canker***, blossom wilt*, brown rot*, peach leaf curl*, stone fruit bacterial leaf spot***, scab*, silver leaf*	***See "Bacterial Diseases" *See "Fungal Diseases"
Pear	Brown rot*, pear canker*, fire blight***, Fabraea leaf spot*, powdery mildew*, rust*, scab*, stony pit virus**	*See "Fungal Diseases" ***See "Bacterial Diseases" **See "Virus/Other Pathogen Diseases"
Persimmon	Armillaria root rot*, botrytis*, leaf spot (see Anthracnose)*, leaf blight*, Phytophthora**, heart rot (see brown rot)*	*See "Fungal Diseases" **See "Virus/Other Pathogen Diseases"
Pomegranate	Anthracnose*, botrytis*, fruit spot*	*See "Fungal Diseases"
Quince	Brown rot*, fire blight***, quick leaf blight (see leaf blight)*, leaf spot (see fungal leaf spot)*, powdery mildew*	*See "Fungal Diseases" **See "Virus/Other Pathogen Diseases
Strawberry	Anthracnose*, botrytis*, fusarium wilt*, leaf spot*, Phytophthora**, powdery mildew*	*See "Fungal Diseases" **See "Virus/Other Pathogen Diseases"

While there are specific treatments for each disease mentioned in the chart, let's address the basics first. Most diseases can be broken down in to three categories: fungal, bacterial, or other—which includes viral and other pathogenic infections. If possible, take the holistic approach first, before reaching for broad spectrum fungicides or chemical treatments. Many imbalances can be corrected, allowing the tree to recover and thrive. Some diseases are incurable, and you may need to take measures to destroy infected biomass and start over.

FUNGAL DISEASES

Fungal diseases are due to overpopulations of a particular strain of fungi or mold. Tight spaces, lack of air circulation, and constantly wet environments tend to be the main causes for this imbalance. To prevent fungal diseases from the onset, plant at recommended distances from other trees, prune to open the canopy, and improve drainage in the soil. If you tried all that and still have problems, here are other options to treat fungal diseases.

1. Remove and destroy affected leaves, fruit, and dead wood from the tree and surrounding soil. Do not compost this biomass.

2. Spread a layer of compost to fortify the tree with fresh microbial biodiversity.

3. Foliar spray the leaves and bark with compost tea to coat surfaces with beneficial microbes. This will combat the pathogens and help restore balance to the tree's ecosystem. Apply as often as every 2 weeks in extreme cases.

4. An added bonus—if the pathogen has a predator (i.e., a bacteria-based spray that eats the fungus) seek out sources of biological remedies and apply them as directed.

5. Redirect water sources to drip only rather than overhead watering if possible, to help prevent the spread of spores.

6. Last resort—some copper fungicides and Bordeaux mixtures are approved for use in organic agriculture, but they are severe; residues can build up in soils to toxic levels, causing problems later on. Sulfur and pyrethrin

Anthracnose attacks a number of different fruit trees, bushes, and ornamental trees.

sprays are also an option as a last resort. Use with extreme caution.

ANTHRACNOSE

There are several different pathogens that can trigger anthracnose, depending on what type of tree it infects. Symptoms include brown spots, sunken spots that spread, dead tips of branches and twigs, and can include leaf drop.

APPLE SCAB

Apple scab (*Venturia inaequalis*) symptoms include dark green or brown spots on leaves, and cracked patches on fruit that make it inedible. The leaves will become yellow and blotchy and then drop. Remove all diseased biomass. As a last resort, copper or pyrethrin sprays will control the disease.

ARMILLARIA ROT

With Armillaria mellea, also known as mushroom disease or oak root rot, you might not see signs of this disease until it has taken over. Symptoms include

Brown rot has many symptoms, none of which bodes well for fruit trees.

dieback and slowed growth, leaf drop, and yellowing leaves. Later damage shows up as white patches of fungi or mushrooms blooming at the base of the trunk or root zone. Once infected, it is basically too late. Remove and destroy the biomass (do not compost) and consider removing surrounding trees as well, since the infection travels through soil mycelia.

BLOSSOM WILT
Symptoms of blossom wilt include premature decay of flowers, fruiting spurs, leaves, and eventually, the fruit itself. It can produce cankers on stems as well. The disease lies dormant over winter and resurrects in spring. Pruning to remove infected tissues is the primary treatment.

BOTRYTIS
There are more than 30 different species of botrytis, and, in some circles, it is considered a parasitic as well as fungal infection. Also known as gray mold, this disease is characterized by dark gray spores that begin as white and spread over the surfaces of fruits, darkening as they grow. Every part of the plant can be infected except for the roots.

BROWN ROT
Brown rot (*Monilinia fructicola*) has similar symptoms to blossom wilt, with mummified fruit as well.

CANE BLIGHT
Cane blight (*Leptospaeria coniothyrium*) symptoms include reddish brown fungal lesions along the length of a cane and dieback of side shoots. Fruits can fail to set as flowers wilt and die. Good drainage, and proper pruning to reduce crowding, will help prevent the disease. Sanitize shears between cuts to prevent spreading it to other canes.

CANE SPOT
See "Anthracnose."

DOWNY MILDEW
While technically an obligate parasite or a "water mold," downy mildew is funguslike so it's listed among the fungal infections that stem from infections of molds from the *Peronospora* or *Plasmopara* genus. Symptoms include fuzzy growth on leaves but these differ in appearance by host species. Downy mildew travels in water, so reduce overhead watering and improve soil drainage. As a last resort, Neem oil or peroxide-based organic sprays will neutralize the infection.

FABRAEA LEAF SPOT
Fabraea leaf spot (*Diplocarpon mespili*) is similar to apple scab; spores infect the tree in spring through summer and it can affect quince as well as pears. Spots are purplish black and eventually enlarge to brown patches. New shoots can be affected as well. The spores overwinter in garden soils, so using best practices for cleanup each season are a must. Organic horticultural oils and kaolin clay applications have been shown to be effective.

FRUIT SPOT
Many fruit spots are connected to anthracnose (See "Anthracnose"), but pomegranate fruit spot can also be caused by *Pseudocercospora punicae* fungus. It triggers small black lesions with no uniform shape that develop larger blotches over time. The damage only affects the surface of the skin, rather than causing damage through the fruit. Good sanitation is required to clear infected biomass each season.

FUNGAL LEAF SPOT
See "Septoria Leaf Spot."

FUSARIUM WILT
Fusarium wilt (*Fusarium oxysporum*) persists in garden soils so crop rotation is necessary if it's found to be affecting plants in one spot. If you know your soil has fusarium wilt, choose resistant varieties ahead of time. It is characterized by yellowing and droopy leaves, cracks near the base of the trunk, and eventual die off. Rather than solarizing soils, use organic bacteria-based soil applications that will outcompete the pathogen.

GUAVA WILT
Gauva wilt is yet another soilborne fungal disease that flares up in soggy soils with poor drainage and wet, humid conditions. Symptoms include yellowing foliage, leaf drop, and slow death of branches. Fruit tends to stop growing, turn hard, and die. Rotting appears near the roots and the bark comes away easily. Consider interplanting with marigolds and turmeric (an experimental practice) to control the disease.

LEAF BLIGHT
There are many different fungi that cause various leaf blights. Lesions can be black, brown, yellow, tan, or gray, and can grow to cover the entire leaf. It can be managed by cutting off and destroying affected branches and leaves. Drip irrigation and well-draining soil will help prevent the disease.

LEAF SPOT
Often called common leaf spot (*Mycospharella fragariae)*, this fungal infestation leaves spots with purple/red edges on leaves and gray to white centers. It spreads when water is splashed onto leaf surfaces, so drip irrigation is recommended. It is mostly cosmetic damage and can go untreated, other than trimming off affected leaves.

MUMMY BERRY

Blueberry fruits develop a gray shriveled appearance due to mummy berry (*Monilinia vaccinii-corymbosi*) spores that travel on the wind, and will continue to live in the soil. Leaves can appear as brown, dried up, or withered at branch tips. Clean up debris in early spring and apply a thick layer of mulch to suppress spore release. Sulfur and copper sprays are not very effective against this disease. Instead, try a citric acid-based organic fungicide as a last resort.

PEACH LEAF CURL

Peach leaf curl (*Taphrina deformans*) appears as discoloration of leaves on stone fruit trees, with puckering curled leaves. Leaves turn red and then brown as the infection takes hold. It can inhibit blossoms and fruit set and damage fruit as a result. It overwinters in buds and bark, so timely applications (prior to budbreak) of compost tea and, if needed, copper- or sulfur-based sprays will curtail the issue. Prune and destroy diseased portions of the tree and amend with compost and worm castings to promote growth.

PEAR CANKER

Affecting pears and sometimes apple trees, pear canker (*Neonectria ditissima*) can grow on scabs, old wounds, and pruning cuts. Symptoms include black sunken patches that spread through the bark. It is more common in soggy soils that don't drain well. Cut out diseased portions of the tree and sanitize between cuts. As a last resort, apply a copper-based spray.

POWDERY MILDEW

Powdery mildew is tricky because each species has a plant-specific relationship. For example, the powdery mildew that attacks your melon patch is a different species than the one that attacks a fruit tree. It's characterized by whitish gray spots on leaf surfaces that spread to cover the entire leaf and stem. Spores drift easily and arrive on coastal breezes or settle in spaces with limited air circulation. It can appear after a period of high humidity followed by heat and can damage fruits as well. Leaves turn crisp and die eventually. Follow instructions for prevention and incorporate Neem oil or other organic horticultural oil if biological treatments don't work first.

RUST

Rust (*Phragmidium* spp.) appears as small, orange, raised specks on leaf surfaces, and eventually spreads to consume the plant. It lives in the soil to return the following year. There are more than 7,000 species of rust that are plant specific, meaning each species of rust targets a specific plant. To reduce its spread, water at soil level instead of overhead, and clean up debris. As a last resort, use a Neem or horticultural oil spray, or a sulfur spray specifically for the type of rust you have.

SCAB

The strain of scab attacking passion fruit (*Cladosporium oxysporum*) is similar to that of plums, but it's different from that of apple scab. The lesions resemble the brown sunken spots that ruin the fruit. Brown spots appear both on leaves and fruit and eventually cause death. The disease overwinters on twigs. Prune to improve air circulation in early spring. Once infected, organic peroxygen-based products or copper sprays can eliminate infection.

SEPTORIA LEAF SPOT

This fungal disease (*Septoria lycopersici*) manifests as brown spots on leaf surfaces between green veins. The spots can have a gray center, be sunken, or have purple margins. Clean up infected debris, as it repopulates for years from diseased material left behind. As a last resort apply a copper spray early in the season to stem off infection.

SHOT HOLE DISEASE

This disease (*Wilsonomyces carpophilus*) appears as red-brown spots on leaves or holes on leaf surfaces on stone fruit trees, followed by leaf drop. It is a blanket term used to describe a number of fungal diseases in combination with a bacterial infection (see "Bacterial Leaf Spot"). Fungicides are not effective on bacterial leaf spot. Trees can go untreated.

SILVER LEAF

Despite its name, silver leaf (*Chondrostereum purpureum*) infects leaves, stems, and trunks of fruit trees. Symptoms include a silver appearance to the leaves followed by stem and branch dieback as wood rots away. Summer pruning helps prevent the disease. Prune and destroy any diseased material, as its spores are airborne.

SMUT

Smut (*Aspergillus* spp.) is a delicacy when it grows on corn, but on figs it's a nuisance. It damages the interior flesh of the fruit, turning it black with a chalky texture. It can be transferred to other fruits on the tree by insects. Implement best practices to remove debris and infected fruits without spreading the spores. Bag and destroy affected biomass. Organic peroxide-based sprays are known to work if the guidelines in "Fungal Diseases" do not adequately reduce or eliminate the problem.

SOOTY MOLD

The main symptom of sooty mold (*Ascomycete* spp.) is the appearance of black sticky dust on leaf surfaces. It is sticky because it forms on top of the honeydew excreted by aphids and doesn't rub off easily. While sooty mold doesn't penetrate leaf surfaces, it does reduce a tree's ability to synthesize nutrients and undergo photosynthesis. See "Sucking Insects" under "Pest Control" to manage the insects that excrete honeydew.

SOUR ROT (SUMMER BUNCH ROT)

This grape disease affects the fruit itself, and is characterized by a black, brown, or green fungus growing on the surface of the grapes. The disease enters wherever damage was done (cracking, birds, or other damage), and tends to appear after heavy rains. Yeasts and bacteria also play a role in causing the physical decay once a plant becomes vulnerable. The skins split and turn brown, sinking into the grape as it decays, while emitting the smell of vinegar. Peroxygen-based organic antimicrobial sprays have shown to be effective, but keep in mind your beneficial microbe population will suffer setbacks as a result.

STEM BLIGHT

Blueberry stem blight (*Botryosphaeria*), also known as dieback, is a vascular disease that turns entire stems brown, including their leaves. It develops in climates with high humidity and frequent rainfall and increases with drought stress. It also can appear as a result of another disease such as *Phytophthora*. Water consistently to eliminate drought stress. See "Botrytis" for additional information.

VERTICILLIUM WILT

This disease attacks a number of plant species and is caused by various Verticilium soilborne fungi. It is characterized by leaves turning yellow, which then eventually wither and fall. Damage travels upward from the base of the plant. Some gardeners recommend solarizing the soil to kill the disease. Biological controls include a few bacterial antagonists, but overall, crop rotation and choosing disease-resistant varieties are recommended.

BACTERIAL DISEASES

Bacterial diseases can be difficult to identify because they don't show immediate symptoms in the way fungal infestations often do. Bacterial diseases also travel on insects, including pollinators, so they spread easily. Many don't have a cure but can be curtailed with proper sanitation, strategic pruning, and timing. Choose disease-resistant varieties if bacterial diseases are known to be an issue in your area. But before all of that, soil health reigns supreme. Compacted soils lead to loss of biological diversity, which triggers imbalances, which invites disease. Keep your soil well fed with compost, compost tea, mulch, and worm castings and your soil biology will outcompete most diseases. They will also keep your soil aerated and well-drained. Remember: Healthy, active soil biology is more important to a tree's survival than nutrients.

Treating Bacterial Diseases

Beyond basic soil care, there are a couple of approaches to treating bacterial diseases. Biostimulant products containing beneficial bacteria strains such as *Bacillus subtilis* and *Bacillus amyloliquefaciens* overpower pathogenic bacteria and fungi that attack root systems. These are available as soil inoculants or labeled as "biofungicide" or "biobactericide" foliar sprays. Lactic acid bacteria have also shown to be "antagonistic" against bacterial diseases, reducing spots and spread of infection. Think about how we use probiotics to boost our own microbiome. You can do the same with your soil and plant surfaces. The higher the diversity of biology, including beneficial bacterial and fungi, the better suited your plants and trees will be to fight off infection.

Follow these guidelines to prevent bacterial diseases and keep them under control.

1. Remove and destroy affected leaves, fruit, and dead wood from the tree and surrounding soil. Do not compost diseased biomass.

2. Spread a layer of compost to fortify the tree with fresh microbial biodiversity.

3. Foliar spray leaves and bark with compost tea to coat surfaces with beneficial microbes. (See the "Brew Compost Tea" sidebar in chapter 2.) This will combat the pathogens and help restore balance to the tree's ecosystem. Apply as often as every 2 weeks in extreme cases.

4. Added bonus—if the pathogen has a predator (i.e., beneficial bacteria or fungi that attack the bad guys) seek out sources of biological remedies and apply them as directed. See the "Treating Bacterial Diseases" sidebar in "Bacterial Diseases" as well.

5. Redirect water sources to drip only rather than overhead watering if possible, to help prevent the spread of disease.

6. Last resort—some horticultural or Neem oils and copper or sulfur bactericides are approved for use in organic agriculture, but they are severe; residues can build up in soils to toxic levels, causing problems later on. Peroxygen (hydrogen peroxide or phosphoric acid-based) sprays are also an option as a last resort. Use with extreme caution.

BACTERIAL BLIGHT

This disease (*Pseudomonas syringae pv. mori*) thrives in wet weather. Brown or black spots first appear on leaf surfaces and look water soaked, with yellow edges. Leaves then wilt and dry up, and shoots develop black streaks. Buds become malformed. Sometimes sap will ooze from cankers on stems, and overall growth is stunted. Prune away dead biomass in late summer or early fall. Apply biostimulant spray as described, or, as a last resort, an organic copper or peroxygen spray.

BACTERIAL CANKER

Many factors can encourage infestation of bacterial canker (*Pseudomonas syringae pv. syringae*) such as improper or untimely pruning, wind and frost damage, and poor soil conditions. It is characterized by stunted growth, leaf spots, dead branches, and oozing of gummy substances. The bark will look discolored and leaves will turn yellow and drop as the limb dies back. Cut out diseased portions of the tree in summer and leave uncovered to dry out.

BACTERIAL SPOT

Symptoms of bacterial spot (*Xanthomonas axonopodis pv. passiflora*) include dark green spots on leaves with puckering between leaf veins. The lesions spread and turn brown, eventually leading to leaf wilt and death. Passion fruits become spotted with lesions that penetrate all the way through to the flesh, causing early drop before the fruit has matured. There is no cure for this disease.

CITRUS CANKER

While a citrus canker (*Xanthomonas axonopodis pv. citri* and *pv. aurantifolii*) infection looks horrible, it mostly affects leaves and the outer rind of citrus fruits. It makes fruit unmarketable, but it shouldn't stop the home gardener from enjoying the fruit. Severe cases cause leaf and fruit drop and branch dieback. As with other bacterial diseases, it loves warm, wet weather. Yellowish pustules turn corky, and symptoms can increase if leafminers are active. The disease can survive for years on damaged plant tissue, so be diligent about removing infected biomass. Some states recommend quarantine (not sharing fruit outside of your own yard) to prevent the spread. Practice good sanitation.

CROWN GALL

Crown gall (*Agrobacterium vitis*) affects grapevines worldwide. It usually appears on or near the graft union as lumpy knobs on the trunk, though some forms manifest as galls higher on vines. The galls become dark and dusty or flaky after turning corky. The disease decreases fruit productivity and can eventually kill the vine and roots entirely. It can survive for upwards of seven years in plant tissues, so vigorous sanitation is recommended when pruning

Bacterial canker in action. Severe pruning and best practices will help keep it at bay.

Fire blight can be kept at bay with aggressive pruning each season.

dead biomass. Pull the plant if the crown is infected and start fresh with disease-resistant varieties. Treat the soil with beneficial nematodes to prevent the damage they cause, which can contribute to infestation of bacterial diseases.

FIRE BLIGHT

This common bacterial disease (*Erwinia amylovora*) appears with watery, dark brown oozing spots, or red-brown wilted leaves and twigs. Entire branches die off in addition to flowers and their stems that wilt and die. The disease overwinters on the tree, and it spreads easily to other branches and trees. Be diligent about pruning away all diseased material either in summer or winter and sanitize pruning tools between cuts. Destroy infected biomass. Bacterial sprays help control infection and as a last resort, use organic copper or peroxygen sprays.

STONE FRUIT BACTERIAL LEAF SPOT

Similar to bacterial spot, stone fruit bacterial leaf spot (*Xanthomonas pruni*) is a strain of the disease that specifically affects stone fruit trees. The disease manifests as deformed leaves and twigs as well as oozing sap from the bark. Deep purple, brown, or black spots appear, developing into shot holes as the center of each spot disintegrates. The spots grow and spread, eventually taking over the leaf surface. The disease overwinters on twigs and can spread to fruits as they develop cankers. Keep the tree well pruned to increase air circulation and cut back all diseased biomass during dry weather.

VIRUSES AND OTHER PATHOGEN DISEASES

Viral and other pathogenic diseases often look like fungal or bacterial infections. They are often parasitic and grow on top of fungi, bacteria, or other hosts that might be also present. Your best bet is to implement preventative measures, including good soil prep, and work toward a healthy soil ecosystem to keep these diseases at bay. The presence of viral infections indicate the impending death of trees or shrubs that are infected. Most plants don't recover. In most cases the best option is to pull the plant or tree and start over in a different location. Below you will find the two most common viruses with suggestions for how to prolong the life of a tree and increase its chances of survival until the end of the season.

MOSAIC VIRUS

There are a number of strains of mosaic virus, including those that affect passion fruits and fig trees. The virus is transmitted to passion fruit by a polyphagous beetle (*Diabrotics speciose*) and to figs by an eriophyd mite (*Aceria fici*). Symptoms present with blotchy leaves that turn yellow-clear between veins with borders of rust. It can also infect branches. New growth is stunted and result in smaller fruits or premature fruit drop. Apply worm castings around the base of plants to ward off mites

PHYTOPHTHORA

Phytophthora is technically algae classified as oomycetes, which affect multiple species of fruit trees and plants by causing root and crown rot, eventually killing a tree. It prefers wet compacted soils, therefore soil preparation to improve drainage, and best practices to inoculate your garden soil with beneficial microbes, will help prevent it. Symptoms appear as red/brown streaks under the bark, oozing sap, and die off of branches. Use drip irrigation and avoid overwatering. Consider applying an organic peroxygen-based spray as a last resort. Some soil specialists recommend applying gypsum around the affected tree followed by a soil drench of compost tea. This has been shown to fight back the disease and allows the tree to recover.

LAST THOUGHTS

This is not goodbye—this is good luck! You are going to learn so much by growing your own fruit. Even if the results are different than you expect, they will get better as your trees and perennial berries mature. You will develop an increased appreciation for the tireless efforts of farmers who bring perfect produce to your table year after year. You will hold fresh harvest in your hand with new respect for the food itself. Homegrown fruits are precious, and worth every ounce of effort. Now, go forth and be fruitful!

APPENDIX A

ROOTSTOCK CHART

Below you will find a list of common rootstocks for different fruits and their traits.

FRUIT	ROOTSTOCK	SPECIFICATIONS
Apple	M27	Very dwarf, no more than 6 ft. [1.8 m] tall. Can stunt some trees in poor soils.
	M9	Dwarf. Most common rootstock used in commercial tree production. Requires staking due to poor anchorage.
	G11	Dwarf. A cross between M26 & Robusta 5. More productive and vigorous than M9.
	M26	Semi-dwarf. Susceptible to fire blight. Need staking.
	M106	Semi-dwarf but vigorous. 65 to 75% of standard size. Resistant to woolly apple aphid. Susceptible to Phytophthora in poor-draining soils.
	M111	Semi-dwarf but vigorous. 80% of standard size. Tolerates poor soils with smaller growth habit. Resistant to woolly apple aphid.
	M25	Standard. Produces at an early age. Not resistant to woolly apple aphid.
Cherry	Gisela 5	Dwarf, but works for patio containers and small gardens.
	Colt	Semi-dwarf but vigorous. Does not tolerate drought conditions, but resistant to root rot. Works well in thin soils.

	Mazzard	Good for coastal gardens. Susceptible to bacterial canker, but resistant to root rot.
Pear	Quince 'C'	Dwarf. Note: Many quince rootstocks are not compatible with some pear varieties. Compatible with 'D'Anjou', 'Comice', 'Flemish Beauty', & 'Swiss Bartlett', but not compatible with 'Bartlett', 'Bosc', 'Seckel', and 'Clapp'. Resistant to root aphids, root rot, and most nematodes.
	Quince 'A'	Semi-dwarf but vigorous. Excellent for bush trees.
	French Seedling	Standard. Good for general use. Tolerates both dry and soggy conditions. Resistant to oak root fungus but susceptible to fire blight.
	Betulaefolia	Standard. Ideal for Asian pears. Produces a large tree in most conditions. Resistant to fire blight, root aphids, and rot, as well as pear decline.
	Old Home × Farmingdale	Dwarf. Compatible with most pears. Fire blight resistant.
Apricot/Peach/ Plum/Nectarine	St. Julian 'A'	Semi-dwarf. Tolerates cold soils. Compatible with all plums, peaches, nectarines, and apricots.
	Citation	Dwarf but vigorous. Great for apricots. Reduced tolerance to bacterial canker, and okay in soggy soils. Root-knot nematode resistant.
	Lovell	Standard. Tolerant of wet soils. Not good in soils with root-rot nematodes.
	Nemaguard	Standard. Resistant to root-rot nematodes. Less tolerant of wet soils than Lovell.

RESOURCES

Find the bibliography of references used while writing this book by chapter at https://Gardenerd.com/Mini-Fruit-Garden/notes.

BOOKS

Buckingham, Alan. *Grow Fruit*. Great Britain: DK Publishing, 2010.

Ingels, Chuck A. Pamela M. Geisel and Maxwell V. Norton editors. *The Home Orchard: Growing Your Own Deciduous Fruit & Nut Trees*. California: University of California Agriculture and Natural Resources Publication #3485, 2007.

Otto, Stella. *The Backyard Berry Book*. Vermont: Chelsea Green Publishing, 1995.

WEBSITES

Dave Wilson Nursery's advice on growing fruit trees – https://www.davewilson.com/home-gardens

The author's website – https://Gardenerd.com

Integrated Pest Management – http://ipm.ucanr.edu/

Permaculture – https://permaculture.org

Biodynamic practices – https://www.biodynamics.com/

Sources for beneficial nematodes and other beneficial insects – Arbico Organics: https://www.arbico-organics.com/, Custom Biologicals: http://living-soils.com/

Compost Tea brewing advice and equipment, and testing services – http://www.earthfort.com/

Tools for pruning and harvesting – Peaceful Valley Farm & Garden Supply: https://www.groworganic.com , Lee Valley Tools: https://www.leevalley.com/en-ca/garden, Felco: https://www.felco.com/, Gardeners Supply: https://www.gardeners.com

ACKNOWLEDGMENTS

The bulk of this book was written while the world collectively grappled with COVID-19. I wrote these pages during the outrage that followed the death of George Floyd, an American Black man killed by police in May 2020; while peaceful protests for justice and riotous looting made headlines; while sirens, helicopters, and curfew alerts were the soundtrack of everyday life in Los Angeles. I was lucky and privileged enough not to have been personally involved or affected, but I am keenly aware that my whiteness afforded me that privilege.

Gardening became an oasis for many during the pandemic. It soothed us when we couldn't stay inside any longer. It sustained us when grocery store shelves were empty. It connected us to something larger than ourselves: nature's bountiful gifts and the common love of coaxing seeds to life. My garden saved my sanity, and this book provided a much-needed distraction from a world turned upside down. I must thank the following for their contributions and support.

To Tom Spellman, for granting me an interview that pulled him away from acres of fruit trees under his care; to David King, for loaning me his grafting knowledge and resources whenever I asked; to JoAnne Trigo of Two Dog Organic Nursery, for pointing me in the direction of Tom Spellman and for her nifty blueberry trick; to Sheri Powell of Compost Teana, for allowing me to double-check Soil Food Web and disease facts with her; to my family and friends, who tolerated my singular focus and next-level stress throughout the writing process; and to Emily Murphy, whose beautiful photography brought these pages to life. And of course, I must thank everyone at Cool Springs Press for shepherding this book into being, particularly Jessica Walliser and Marissa Giambrone, who worked with me every step of the way.

Gardening may not be the answer to all our problems, but it sure makes life better every single day. My mission is to save the world, one garden at a time. May this book help you create an oasis for your own benefit and for the benefit of all humankind.

ABOUT THE AUTHOR

Christy Wilhelmi empowers people to grow their own food, to be more self-reliant, and to reduce pollution and waste, one garden at a time. Christy is founder of Gardenerd, the ultimate resource for garden nerds, where she publishes newsletters, her popular blog, and top-ranked podcasts. She also specializes in small-space, organic vegetable garden design and consulting. She holds regular organic gardening classes in California and offers tips on her YouTube channel.

Christy was a board member of Ocean View Farms Organic Community Garden in Mar Vista, California, for over 20 years, and gardens almost entirely with heirloom vegetables. Between 70 to 80 percent of her family's produce comes from her garden of fewer than 300 square feet. Her writing has appeared in many publications, and she is author of *Gardening for Geeks* (Fox Chapel Publishing), *400+ Tips for Organic Gardening Success: A Decade of Tricks, Tools, Recipes, and Resources from Gardenerd.com* (Amazon Digital), and *Garden Variety: A Novel.*

INDEX

Q

quince, 47, 132–133, 152, 162, 174, 177, 185

R

raccoons, 169
raspberries
    about, 90
    chill hours and, 47
    diseases of, 173
    growing, 86
    planting, 88–89
    primocanes and floricanes, 87
    pruning, 91
    seasons of, 85
    thornless bush, 19
    wandering, *13*
rats, 169–170
red blotch, 173
repellents, deer, 165
reversion disease, 173
ripening, successive, 15–16
root flares, 73, 74
root rot, 127, 173, 185
roots, girdled, 27
rootstock, 25–27, 184–185
rot diseases, 174
'Royal Lee' cherry, 52, 60
rust (*Phragmidium* spp.), 173, 174, 178

S

sanitizing pruning equipment, 141, 142
scab, 48, 174, 178
scale, 171–172
scions, 25, 56, 59–64, 66, 68
'Seckel' pears, 52, 185
selection, fruit tree, 42, 44–48, 52
self-fruitful trees, 52
semi-dwarf rootstock, 26, 184–185
Septoria leaf spot (*Septoria lycopersici*), 173, 174, 178
shot hole disease (*Wilsonomyces carpophilus*), 173, 179
shrub berries. *See* bush berries
silver leaf (*Chondrostereum purpureum*), 173, 174, 179
size, tree, 14, 25
smut (*Aspergillus* spp.), 173, 179
soil
    acidifying, 96
    clay-type, 31, 33
    container, 78
    lines on trees, 73, 74, 117

soil conditions
    for apples, 129
    for apricots, 133
    for blueberries, 96
    for cane berries, 88–89
    for cherries, 134
    for dragon fruit, 107
    for gages, 137
    for gooseberries and currants, 96
    for grapes, 113
    for nectarines, 134
    for peaches, 134
    for pears, 130
    for plums, 137
    for quince, 133
    for strawberries, 101
Soil Food Web, 30–31
soil preparation
    about, 30–33
    to deter pests, 162, 168, 171
    diseases and, 180, 182
soil test kit, home, 121–122
sooty mold (*Ascomycete* spp.), 173, 179
sour rot, 173, 179
sow bug (*Oniscidea*), 102, 168
spiders, 163
Spinosad, 167
squirrels, 169
staking, 76–77
stem blight (*Botryosphaeria*), 173, 179
stone fruit bacterial leaf spot (*Xanthomonas pruni*), 174, 182
stone fruits, 14, 43, 45, 133–137, 164, 167, 178–179, 182
    See also specific stone fruits
stony pit virus, 174
strawberries
    about, 100
    bare-root, 101
    chill hours and, 47
    choosing, 100
    diseases of, 174
    feeding and harvesting, 102, 104
    mulching and, 102
    pests of, 164
    placement of, 19, 85
    planting, 101
    pruning, 104–105
    revitalizing, 104
subtending, 152

suckers, 142, 149, 159
sulfur, 126, 128
sulfur sprays, 175, 178, 180
summer bunch rot. *See* sour rot
summer pruning, 148–149
sunblotch viroid, 173
sunscald, 148
'Swiss Bartlett' pears, 185

T

tags, grafting, 59
tape, grafting, 61, 62, 66
T-budding, 64
thinning fruit, 127
thorns, pomegranate, 159
The Three Ds (dead, diseased, disorderly), 98, 141–142, 150, 152–153, 155–156
tools, grafting, 61
tools, pruning, 150
traps, 165–166, 169, 170
tree guards, 76, 165
tree shapes, 139–141
trellis plants, 107, 110

U

underwatering, 127

V

vertical gardening, 19
verticillium wilt, 173, 174, 179
vines, 20, 110–115, 117–119
voles, 170

W

wasps, 162–163
watering
    apples, 129
    apricot trees, 133
    container trees, 39
    dragon fruit, 107
    grapes, 114
    overwatering, 121, 126–127
    pears, 132
    quince, 133
    underwatering, 127
    See also irrigation
watersprouts, 149, 151
wax for grafting trees, 61, 62
wedges, 61
whiteflies, 171–172
woodiness, 174
wooly apple aphids, 184
worm castings, 79, 81, 101, 122, 126, 172, 180, 182
worms, 31, 126, 165